HEALING WATERS

A Bible Study on Forgiveness, Grace, and Second Chances

Based on The Inn at Shining Waters Series

With MELODY CARLSON

ABINGDON PRESS
Nashville

CONTENTS

INTRODUCTION

It's impossible to pass through life without experiencing some kind of hurt or loss. We all need healing at different points in our lives, and often the path to healing is paved in some form of forgiveness and grace.

Healing Waters invites us on a journey to healing, a journey in which our God, the Lord who heals, walks with us and invites us to experience His love and mercy every step of the way. Together we will walk the roads of forgiveness and grace, learning how to embrace them for ourselves and for our relationships. We will learn how to restore broken relationships and how to live in life-giving community. And we will celebrate God, the giver of second chances—the One who transforms us and blesses us with surprises and new beginnings.

What makes this study unique is that it uses Christian fiction as a backdrop to explore the sometimes complex and often surprising journey to healing. Just as Jesus used stories (parables) to teach important principles, sometimes fiction can inspire and change us as well. Through the characters and stories of The Inn at Shining Waters Series, we will consider the need for forgiveness and mercy in our lives and discover the important role that second chances and new beginnings play in healing our relationships and our spirits. The hope is that this refreshing approach of combining Bible study with narrative storytelling will not only enrich and enhance your study of God's Word but also help you to better understand and apply what you're learning in your own life as you relate to the characters and their experiences.

Everything needed to complete the study is provided in this book and your weekly group experience, in which you will watch a short video segment providing background information and insights into the characters, stories, and themes. *Reading the novels is not required.* However, if you feel you would enjoy reading the novels in tandem with the study (each is a quick read), you may find this enhances your overall experience.

Optional Reading Plan
Book 1: *River's Song* — Weeks 1-3
Book 2: *River's Call* — Weeks 4-5
Book 3: *River's End* — Weeks 6-7

> What makes this study unique is that it uses Christian fiction as a backdrop to explore the sometimes complex and often surprising journey to healing.

Reading the
novels is
not required.
However, if you
feel you would
enjoy reading the
novels in tandem
with the study
(each is a quick
read), you may
find this enhances
your overall
experience.

Whether reading the books themselves or only the excerpts and character sketches provided in this book, over the next eight weeks you will come to know three generations of women (Anna, her daughter Lauren, and granddaughter Sarah—all descendants of the Siuslaw Indians) and the life challenges and healing journeys each experiences over several decades of life. Each woman's journey is connected in some way to the beautiful Siuslaw River, located along Oregon's Pacific coast, which links her to her heritage and serves as a place of healing. As you encounter their stories, you will be exploring the themes of forgiveness, grace, relationships, community, transformation, new beginnings, and the goodness of God—all through a biblical framework. The foundational text for the study is Psalm 103, which is a beautiful passage of Scripture describing God's love and provision for us and celebrating how only God can make us whole.

While writing these novels, I recognized how my main character (Anna) was blessed with an exceptionally gracious spirit. Despite the heartbreaks and difficulties in her life, she realized her need to forgive and move on. As a result she experienced personal healing and eventually became an instrument of healing for others. Anna exemplified how grace and healing go hand in hand. And although a fictional character, she became a role model for me. I'd like to be more like Anna.

As you'll see, this book is divided into three sections, each corresponding to one of the three novels. A summary of each novel precedes the beginning of its section, along with several character sketches. This introductory material is titled "Before You Begin." You will want to read this material before delving into the weekly readings in that section.

Each week begins with a Scripture for the week and an excerpt from the related novel, setting the stage for the five readings that follow. Each day's reading may be completed in approximately twenty to thirty minutes and follows this format:

Read God's Word	A Scripture focus for the day.
Reflect and Respond	Reflections on the day's topic featuring insights from Scripture, excerpts from the novels, and questions for reflection and response.
Talk to God	A prayer to read or use as a starting point in a time of personal prayer.
As You Go	A suggestion for the day—a question to ponder, a Scripture to consider, or some action to take.

The interactive format of the daily readings guides you through the material, providing questions for reflection with space for writing your responses. You will have the opportunity to share some of these responses when you gather with your small group. Writing your thoughts in the space provided will prepare you for the weekly group sessions as well as capture the insights you are gaining on your journey. As a writer, I'm well aware of the power of putting words to paper. It can be an effective step toward self-discovery and healing.

I am honored to walk alongside you as we travel this road together. I pray that God blesses you with his love, mercy, and grace each step of the way.

Melody Carlson

THEME 1

Healing Through Forgiveness and Grace

River's Song

BEFORE YOU BEGIN

Book Summary: *River's Song*

The year is 1959. Following her mother's funeral, widow Anna Larson returns to her childhood home to sort out her parents' belongings. Situated on a picturesque coastal estuary in Oregon, Anna's unique family home is filled with an assortment of memories—some lovely, some difficult. Anna had hoped that her daughter, Lauren, who had just graduated from high school, would join her on the trip home, but their strained relationship kept them at arms' length from each other. At first Anna felt guilty about leaving Lauren behind, but her mother-in-law, Eunice, made it perfectly clear that she had everything under control—including Lauren. Anna was beginning to feel that she was no longer needed there anyway.

Anna comes to the river of her youth feeling empty and lost, but she soon remembers how much she loves being on the water and revels in its healing properties. Anna is also flooded with memories of her Grandma Pearl, who was a full Siuslaw Indian. Though Anna's mother had rejected her Native American heritage for a more modern lifestyle, Anna had loved being with her grandmother, learning how to make traditional baskets and listening to her ancient stories. She finds comfort in her grandmother's objects and artifacts scattered throughout the home, the connection to her past growing stronger minute by minute. As she settles in, Anna meets Hazel Chenowith, an energetic grandmother who has travelled to the river to research the Siuslaw Indians. Gathering information for her doctoral thesis, Hazel is ecstatic to discover Anna's heritage, and Anna invites her to stay in her grandmother's old cabin while Hazel collects information.

Soon Anna is feeling better than she has in years, surrounded by Hazel and Babette, her mother's old friend who lives nearby and takes Anna under her wing. As Anna begins to reconnect with her heritage and the rustic ways of river living, she begins to realize how miserable she has been over the past years, living with her wealthy mother-in-law, Eunice, and dealing with her relentless verbal abuse. Eunice had been livid when her son, Adam, married Anna, and when Adam returned home from war, broken in body and in spirit, Anna and Adam had moved into Eunice's home with their young daughter, Lauren, where Anna had cared for Adam until his tragic death. Though Anna and Lauren remained in the home after Adam's death, Anna quickly became subservient to the sharp-tongued and manipulative Eunice, whose dominance seemed inescapable.

But here now, on the river, Anna begins to hope and to dream of a different life, one that is lived on her own terms and celebrates the healing environment of the river. With Hazel's encouragement, Anna realizes her skills in hospitality and begins to transform the beautiful house and property into an inn—a place that can be a healing retreat for many, many people. Then, when Hazel's contractor son, Clark, comes to visit, Anna's heart is awakened. Clark's kind, encouraging manner steals her heart, and she begins to open herself up to the possibility of being worthy of another's love. Their relationship grows, and when Clarke proposes marriage, Anna is eager to accept, overjoyed by the promises of her new life.

By transforming her old family home into Shining Waters Inn, Anna creates a place of healing—a place where guests experience peace, grace, and new beginnings for themselves—while transforming her own life and growing into the woman that God intended her to be.

Character Sketches

Anna

Born in the early twenties, Anna lived a quiet, protected life with her two loving parents and grandmother on the banks of the Siuslaw River. Anna's mother, a Siuslaw Indian who'd been born and "educated" on the reservation and experienced the hardships and horrors there, grew to resent her Native American roots and chose to live as a "white woman" and married a Scandinavian immigrant. When the grandmother returned to her "old ways," Anna's mother came to resent her as well. However, Anna enjoyed a rich and interesting relationship with her grandmother until the grandmother died when Anna was around twelve. Anna grew into an intelligent and beautiful woman. Tall and strong and independent, she was just starting college when she caught the eye of Adam Gunderson who persuaded her to elope before the onset of World War II. Anna's only child, Lauren, is born shortly before Adam goes to war, and Anna feels trapped by Eunice, her mother-in-law. She feels even more oppressed when Adam returns with serious injuries and later takes his own life. During Lauren's "growing up" years Eunice wields her control over Anna and Lauren, treating Anna like a slave and Lauren like a princess. It's not until Anna's mother passes away (shortly before Lauren goes to college) that Anna makes her break from Eunice.

Hazel

Born in the late 1800s, Hazel grew up with the belief that women were equal to men. Unfortunately the society she lived in seldom agreed. However, Hazel entered college and was nearly finished when she became pregnant with Clark. Unfortunately, Clark's father didn't wish to marry. So, Hazel began to raise her son with the help of her mother while continuing her education and career. Hazel has one less than happy marriage, but she eventually turns her attention to her career as an anthropology professor and to raising her child. By the time she meets Anna, she is working toward her doctoral degree, writing a dissertation on Northwest coastal tribes and folklore stories. Delighted to meet Anna and discover the old stories of Anna's grandmother, a firm bond forms between the two women. Hazel becomes a mentor and mother figure to Anna. And, eventually Hazel's son Clark enters the picture too. A match made in heaven (or by Hazel) ensues.

Clark

About five years Anna's senior, Clark (raised by Hazel) grew up in a non-conventional home as an independent thinker. Although he earned a degree in law, his stint in the Army Air Corp during World War II (dropping bombs) instilled a desire to return home and "build things instead of destroy them." Subsequently he becomes a contractor and occasionally uses his legal expertise to help others. Clark's first wife didn't appreciate his transition from attorney to carpenter, and the marriage disintegrated. However, Clark remained committed to his son Marshall, maintaining a healthy relationship despite the failed marriage. Eventually, his wife remarried, selecting a more "successful" man. By the time Clark enters Anna's world, he's weary of building post–World War II houses, and he wants something more challenging. He not only falls in love with Anna but the river, and her vision for running an inn as well.

Babette

Babette (of uncertain age, but much older than she appears) was a good friend to Anna's parents and even helped them to run the store on the river. As a beautiful young woman, Babette emigrated from France and lived in San Francisco, where she married an old, unsuccessful miner, and after he passed away she married a second miner and businessman (Bernard) who was successful. Bernard passed away not long after coming to the river, leaving Babette well-off but alone. Her generosity and cheerful spirit gained many friendships along the river. And when Anna returns to her roots, Babette takes her under her wing and proves as valuable as family.

WEEK 1
THE JOURNEY TO HEALING

Scripture for the Week

Let my whole being bless the LORD!
Let everything inside me
bless his holy name!
Psalm 103:1

Excerpt from *River's Song*, Chapters 1 and 2

In twenty years' time, nothing had changed on the river. Or so it seemed. Although mid June, the sky was gloomy, the color of a weathered tin roof, and the river, a few shades darker, was tinged with mossy green. The surface of the water was serene, barely moving with the ebb tide, and the sounds of birds and churning boat motor were muffled, hushed by the low-slung clouds....

[Anna] pushed the door open with her foot and reached for her suitcase. Taking a deep breath, unsure of what to expect, she went inside. It had only been six days since her mother had died right here in this house. She knew that Mrs. Thorne, a neighbor from upriver, had stopped by last week to share a bucket of clams, but had found her mother on the kitchen floor. The doctor said she'd been dead for a day or two, but had in all likelihood died instantly. Probably a stroke or heart attack. No need for an autopsy, he'd said, nothing suspicious about a sixty-nine-year-old woman dying in her own kitchen. Anna swallowed hard and closed the door behind her. She set her suitcase on a straight back chair and looking around, she sighed in relief. Thankfully, all signs of the recent tragedy had been removed. Everything looked scrubbed clean and neat with even a vase of wild snapdragons on the kitchen table, probably from Mrs. Thorne, or maybe Babette. River folks were like that—they looked out for each other.

Anna set the box of food on the kitchen table, putting the perishable items in the old icebox, which was cold as well as recently cleaned. Now she went straight to her mother's beloved piano. She gently ran her fingers over the keys, playing a scale. Still in tune, but the sound was slightly jarring in the otherwise silent house. Daddy had sent for the upright piano when Anna was around four. It was to be a Christmas present for Mother. Anna still remembered looking on in awe as Daddy and three other men carried the enormous crate from the dock and into the house. She stood in the doorway, watching as Daddy used a crowbar to pry big pieces of wood from the crate. She had been told to keep watch in case Mother came up while he was unpacking it, but Mother had more than enough to keep her busy that day with last-minute holiday shoppers flocking into the tiny store. Anna had hoped that there was a pony inside the big box, and was slightly dismayed when a tall brown piano appeared instead. Mother had cried when she saw it. Then to Anna's amazement she sat down and played—beautifully. It turned out that Mother had taken lessons (in exchange for housekeeping) as a child. And her dream had been to teach Anna to play as well. Consequently, almost every day after the arrival of the piano, Anna was subjected to a long hour's worth of lessons and practice.

She studied a silver-framed photo on the piano. She had seen it hundreds of times, but suddenly it was like seeing it for the first time. It had been Easter Sunday when her family had posed for a neighbor in front of their store before church, all three of them in their Sunday best. Anna must've been around seven or eight, because it was before the Great Depression and the last time she would have pretty shoes like those for a while. The shoes were soft white leather with dainty straps and not a bit practical for life on the Siuslaw River, but Daddy had thought they were pretty and brought them home for her just a few days earlier.

Although the photo was black and white, in her mind's eye she could see it in color, and her dress was a delightful robin's egg blue with several layers of ruffles on the skirt. Mother had made it for her. Anna's long dark hair was pulled back with an oversized bow that matched the dress. Even as a girl, it was easy to see that Anna would take after her father in build and height, already resembling a gangling colt, and her face took on angles not normally seen in the Siuslaw people. But her eyes were dark and clear and full of life. Eyes that Anna had not seen in years.

The dark-eyed girl in the photo was smiling happily. Life had been good for them. She was her parent's little pearl, and the world was her oyster. Anna's focus moved to her mother. How incredibly young she looked! Almost like a girl herself. Her mother stood nearly a foot shorter than her six-foot-tall husband, but unlike many of her race, she was neither squat nor heavy. Her facial features were traditional Siuslaw—broad nose, big dark eyes, and full lips with the corners turned slightly up—but her eyes were downcast, as if she were too shy to look straight into the lens of the camera.

In this photo, Mother's sleek black hair had been recently cut into a stylish short bob. Anna could still remember the horrified look on Daddy's face when Mother had come home from town after having her long tresses cut. He had lamented the loss for some time, then must have noticed Mother's somber face close to tears, and he quickly recovered, reassuring her that she looked very nice in her new "boy's" hair. Mother wasn't a beauty, but she was attractive in a wholesome way. Her dress, like all their clothing, had been sewn by her. It was an off-white linen, straight and sensible, not unlike the fashion of the times, and her lace-up shoes were sturdy and sensible. Her appearance was exactly what one would expect for the wife of a store proprietor in the late twenties; except, of course, that she was Indian.

Anna's gaze moved over to Daddy and she smiled. He stood ramrod straight, looking directly into the camera as if he were the proudest man on the river. Not the kind of pride associated with arrogance, but happy and satisfied with life. His jacket was slung casually over his arm, and he had on his good suspenders, or braces, as he called them. His long narrow tie seemed to exaggerate his height, but Daddy had never been a bow-tie man. But it was his smile that stopped her. Big and broad and sincere. It was that smile that brought people into the store even if they didn't need to make a purchase. Old Mrs. O'Neil had once commented that "Oscar Larson's smile was just like sunshine." And with overcast days so common to the Oregon coast, a slice of sunshine could be a priceless commodity indeed.

After all these years, Anna would still agree with Mrs. O'Neil. How she missed that sunny smile and those clear blue eyes that crinkled at the edges—Daddy's whole face seemed to light up when he smiled. People used to say that Anna had her father's smile. Certainly, no one would make that claim anymore. Time and trials had worn it away. Just last week her mother-in-law had commented that perhaps the reason Anna was approaching forty without facial wrinkles was because she rarely showed emotion. Anna might have received that as a compliment, but her mother-in-law quickly added, "I guess that's just the way it is with your people. I've always thought that Indian faces look as if they're carved in stone." Anna had wondered if her mother-in-law's heart might also be carved in stone. But, out of habit she had held her tongue. She had long since learned that to respond to her mother-in-law's continual barbs only made matters worse.

Anna replaced the photo and moved to the north windows that looked out over the river. She slid back the faded blue-and-white gingham café curtains that her mother had sewn before the war. For a long time she stood there, mesmerized by the watery world outside of the north window. Eventually the deluge eased itself into a steady drizzle and Anna continued to stare out across the river. Her river. Even on a gray and rainy day, there was a soothing quality to the slow moving water. It was constant and dependable, ebbing and flowing with the tide, yes, but continually moving westward on its journey to the sea. The Siuslaw had always filled her with a sense of peace. A calm reassurance that life would continue. But how long had it been since she'd experienced that kind of peace in her own life? Was it possible she could ever experience it again?

How many times had she stood in this exact spot, looking out over her peaceful river world, thinking that it would never change? Truly, the river never did change. Outside of its seasonal rhythms and tidal flows, its song remained the same. A timeless melody of blue and green, water and trees, sunshine and moonlight, rain and wind. And for a brief moment she felt as if nothing in the entire world had changed.

And yet, she knew, nothing was the same.

· · · · · · ·

"Truly, the river never did change. Outside of its seasonal rhythms and tidal flows, its song remained the same."

DAY 1: COME TO THE WELL

Read God's Word

Jesus had to go through Samaria. He came to a Samaritan city called Sychar, which was near the land Jacob had given to his son Joseph. Jacob's well was there. Jesus was tired from his journey, so he sat down at the well. It was about noon.

A Samaritan woman came to the well to draw water. Jesus said to her, "Give me some water to drink." His disciples had gone into the city to buy him some food.

The Samaritan woman asked, "Why do you, a Jewish man, ask for something to drink from me, a Samaritan woman?" (Jews and Samaritans didn't associate with each other.)

Jesus responded, "If you recognized God's gift and who is saying to you, 'Give me some water to drink,' you would be asking him and he would give you living water."

The woman said to him, "Sir, you don't have a bucket and the well is deep. Where would you get this living water? You aren't greater than our father Jacob, are you? He gave this well to us, and he drank from it himself, as did his sons and his livestock."

Jesus answered, "Everyone who drinks this water will be thirsty again, but whoever drinks from the water that I will give will never be thirsty again. The water that I give will become in those who drink it a spring of water that bubbles up into eternal life."

The woman said to him, "Sir, give me this water, so that I will never be thirsty and will never need to come here to draw water!"

Jesus said to her, "Go, get your husband, and come back here."

The woman replied, "I don't have a husband."

"You are right to say, 'I don't have a husband'," Jesus answered. *"You've had five husbands, and the man you are with now isn't your husband. You've spoken the truth."*

The woman said, "Sir, I see that you are a prophet. Our ancestors worshipped on this mountain, but you and your people say that it is necessary to worship in Jerusalem."

Jesus said to her, "Believe me, woman, the time is coming when you and your people will worship the Father neither on this mountain nor in Jerusalem. You and your people worship what you don't know; we worship what we know because salvation is from the Jews. But the time is coming—and is here!—when true worshippers will worship in spirit and truth. The Father looks for those who worship him this way. God is spirit, and it is necessary to worship God in spirit and truth."

The woman said, "I know that the Messiah is coming, the one who is called the Christ. When he comes, he will teach everything to us."

Jesus said to her, "I Am—the one who speaks with you."

Just then, Jesus' disciples arrived and were shocked that he was talking with a woman. But no one asked, "What do you want?" or "Why are you talking with her?" The woman put down her water jar and went into the city. She said to the people, "Come and see a man who has told me everything I've done! Could this man be the Christ?" They left the city and were on their way to see Jesus.

John 4:4-30

Reflect and Respond

It was a normal day for the woman who came to Jacob's well to draw water. Scholars theorize that the woman was an outcast—that she came to the well to draw water in the heat of the day, at noon, long after all the other women had left. Maybe she wanted to avoid the nasty glances and not-so-hushed gossip from the other women in the village. She wanted to go about her day in peace, but this day she went to the well unaware that her life was about to change. A Jewish man walked up and sat down, and he spoke to her. This surprised her; Jews and Samaritans hated one another and actively went out of their way to avoid one another.

But Jesus didn't avoid her. Instead he looked her in the eyes. There was no anger or sarcasm in his voice, only a knowing look and words that penetrated her soul. That day God surprised her—with truth and with an invitation.

I remember when God first surprised me. I was in high school and had proclaimed myself an atheist several years earlier. I think it was actually my secret cry for God to show me He was real. Thankfully, He did reveal Himself to me when I heard the gospel message (for the first time ever), and it miraculously resonated in my soul. I knew it was real and true and just the lifeline I needed. I went from atheist to believer in an amazing moment—and I've never turned back.

Have you ever been surprised by God? What happened?

What does Christ offer the woman?

What did he mean when he offered her "living water"?

We don't know much about the woman who was at the well that day, but Jesus knew everything about her. Jesus' question about her husband was not a casual inquiry but an invitation to offer him the hurts in her life. So, she admitted that she did not have a husband. "You are right to say, 'I don't have a husband,'" Jesus answered. "You've had five husbands, and the man you are with now isn't your husband. You've spoken the truth" (John 4:17-18).

> I remember when God first surprised me. I was in high school and had proclaimed myself an atheist several years earlier. I think it was actually my secret cry for God to show me He was real.

This woman's situation may be nothing like ours, but it's not hard to see ourselves in her. Many of us have spoken half-truths and lies to ourselves and others in order to cover up our pain. We've said, "It's no big deal. I'm over it. That was a long time ago." Many of us, like Anna, have tried to fade into the background of our lives and communities, believing there are no second chances. We are afraid to acknowledge how big and deep our hurts are for fear that we will be judged and rejected—that what we've done and what we've experienced will be too much.

But it's not too much for God. Though we may be afraid to speak the truth, God already knows it, and God invites us to come just the same and drink living water. God is not unaware of our pasts. God knows the depth of our sin and pain and wants us to run to Him for healing.

> If we are believers in Christ and trust in his redeeming work on the cross, none of our past sins holds us back from being accepted and forgiven. We are chosen and favored, and God will never let us go.

How does acknowledging our pain and hurt bring those things out of the darkness and into the light where they can be known and healed?

When God nudges you to acknowledge a sin or a hurt, how do you tend to react?

Read Luke 12:7. How does this verse speak to God's knowledge of you?

Read John 15:16. What does this verse say about God's pursuit of us?

Our journeys are littered with heartache and healing, pain and purpose. Just as Jesus blessed the Samaritan woman with a revelation of who He is, so He has revealed himself to us through his Word and the Holy Spirit. If we are believers in Christ and trust in His redeeming work on the cross, none of our past sins holds us back from being accepted and forgiven. We are chosen and favored, and God will never let us go. We can boldly proclaim God's favor, as the psalmist in Psalm 103:1: "Let my whole being bless the LORD and never forget all his good deeds: how God forgives all your sins, heals all your sickness, saves your life from the pit, crowns you with faithful love and compassion, and satisfies you with plenty of good things" (vv. 2-5).

Jesus told the woman at the well that he was the long-awaited Messiah; He had not yet revealed this truth even to His disciples. What do you think she felt when Jesus told her that He was the one so many generations had been waiting for?

What healing have you been waiting for in your life? How is God inviting you to experience Him in the waiting?

Talk to God

Dear Lord, I am that woman at the well. I have turned to lesser gods to fulfill the needs and desires of my heart. I have spoken half-truths and lies. Thank you for offering me the well that never runs dry. Thank you for the invitation to know you and to be healed in the way that only you can. Give me the faith and courage to follow you. Amen.

As You Go

Spend time in prayer today, asking God to reveal to you the areas in your life that need to be healed. Ask for sensitivity to God's leading and courage to follow Him to healing.

DAY 2: THE HIDDEN MOURNING

Read God's Word

"Examine me, God! Look at my heart! Put me to the test! Know my anxious thoughts! Look to see if there is any idolatrous way in me, then lead me on the eternal path!"

Psalm 139:23-24

Reflect and Respond

Returning to her childhood home for the first time in twenty years, Anna is unsure. Though the place feels familiar and welcoming, Anna is overcome by memories as she returns to this place that has so shaped her life.

Excerpt from *River's Song,* Chapter 3

With hungry eyes, Anna looked around her childhood home. Thankful that Mother had changed so little over the past two decades, she was relieved to see that even the furnishings were in the same places. Maybe that was Mother's way of preserving the past. Even the smells were the same. Pungently comforting. The ever-present mustiness that came from living near water; the faint aroma of sweet cedar from the wood paneling on the ceiling; the smoky smell from the fireplace that never drafted properly in a windstorm, and all tinged by the lingering fragrance of dried lavender.

Life had been so sweet and simple then. Anna sighed. If only it were so simple now. She looked out the window again. At the present moment, her river didn't look any more like the Shining Waters than she felt like an Indian princess. She set [her grandmother's] woven basket down and sank onto the old, familiar camel hair sofa, pulling a shabby pink and green knitted afghan over her legs. She fingered the crocheted throw with sadness. Already it was falling apart, whether from moths or too much use, and it would soon be a useless pile of pink and green yarn bits. And yet her mother's own hands had meticulously hooked each loop on this blanket. Anna still remembered how, so many years ago, after several months of crocheting each evening, her mother had draped the pink and green fruit of her labors over the back of this very sofa with such pride.... And now the blanket looked so shabby and pathetic and stringy. Compared to the beautiful Indian baskets on the coffee table, the afghan seemed rather silly... and useless... and sad.

And for the first time, in a very long time, Anna cried.

• • • • • • •

"I'm in mourning" is not a phrase that you're likely to hear from the people in your life. And yet it is a phrase that aptly describes what Anna was going through—and what many of us are going through, as well.

Though mourning is usually associated with the death of a loved one, we go through the same emotional process of grieving when we feel the loss of what once was or what could have been.

Anna, who in her youth never really understood her mother, grieves for the relationship the two of them never really had. She mourns the time in her life when she believed anything was possible, when life was simpler and more certain.

Mourning is a part of each of our journeys in some shape or form, flowing in and out of our lives as we grow and change. Perhaps you have lost someone you loved who played a big role in your life. Maybe you moved away from your home and your friends and family and are starting over in a new town. Perhaps you've lost your innocence or your independence or a friendship that you cherished. Or maybe your life just isn't what you always dreamed it would be.

We all experience loss in our lives, but when it happens, we don't always know how to process it or what to do with the strong emotions we feel as a result.

What do you think about when you hear the word *mourning?*

Is mourning a process you've been through?

When you feel a loss in your life, how do you typically respond?

Many psychologists say that there are five stages of grief (or loss): denial, anger, bargaining, depression, and acceptance.[1] Have you ever experienced any of these stages? If so, what were the circumstances surrounding that time in your life?

Are you experiencing any strong emotions that you don't quite know how to handle? Maybe you're dealing with anger or depression or anxiety or restlessness. How might these emotions be pointing you toward some loss or disappointment in your life that you need to mourn?

We may be afraid of our strong emotions, but God is not. Throughout Scripture we see God comforting, reassuring, and healing the hearts and minds of those who love him. When we are overwhelmed and confused, God is present and patient, diligently caring for us.

In today's Scripture from Psalm 139, we find a plea for a thorough heart examination. The psalmist cries out, "Examine me, God! Look at my heart! Put me to the test! Know my anxious thoughts! Look to see if there is any idolatrous way in me, then lead me on the eternal path!" (vv. 23-24). God knows the extent of our pain and grief and how to lead us through it.

> We may be afraid of our strong emotions, but God is not. Throughout Scripture we see God comforting, reassuring, and healing the hearts and minds of those who love Him.

In his play *Macbeth*, Shakespeare writes, "Give sorrow words. The grief that does not speak whispers the o're-fraught heart, and bids it break." How can our unspoken, or unacknowledged, grief affect our hearts and minds?

Read the following verses. What comfort or encouragement does each offer for times of mourning or grieving?

Isaiah 41:10

Matthew 5:3-4

John 11:35

1 Peter 5:7

Ecclesiastes 3:1, 4 says, "There's a season for everything and a time for every matter under the heavens: . . . a time to weep and a time to laugh, a time to mourn and a time to dance." Though mourning is not a quick or easy process, Scripture encourages us that "God works all things together for good for the ones who love God, for those who are called according to his purpose" (Romans 8:28).

Although I haven't lost too many loved ones to death, I am well acquainted with grief. Both of my sons have suffered some devastating challenges and setbacks, unexpected events that have broken this mother's heart...including a serious diagnosis of a mental disorder for one and a struggle with addiction for the other. The only way I could survive these ordeals was to fall on God and to trust Him for the outcome. Thankfully, time passed and life eventually improved for everyone.

Is there some hurt or loss in your life that you need to acknowledge and mourn? If so, what is it?

If there's something you've been ignoring or avoiding, how are you currently dealing with it? How is it affecting your heart and life?

How might God be calling you into mourning so that you can walk through this hurt or loss and, on the other side, be able to dance again?

Talk to God

"Investigate my life, O God, find out everything about me; Cross-examine and test me, get a clear picture of what I'm about; See for yourself whether I've done anything wrong—then guide me on the road to eternal life" (Psalm 139:23-24 THE MESSAGE). Amen.

As You Go

As we'll learn in the next few weeks, God's grace is big enough to cover every grief and sorrow we have, and God wants us to experience His grace and love even as we are walking through struggle and pain. Today, be reminded that God walks with you in your journey and can be trusted with your heart.

DAY 3: GOD IS ENOUGH

Read God's Word

When they came back down the mountain to the other disciples, they saw a huge crowd around them, and the religion scholars cross-examining them. As soon as the people in the crowd saw Jesus, admiring excitement stirred them. They ran and greeted him. He asked, "What's going on? What's all the commotion?"

A man out of the crowd answered, "Teacher, I brought my mute son, made speechless by a demon, to you. Whenever it seizes him, it throws him to the ground. He foams at the mouth, grinds his teeth, and goes stiff as a board. I told your disciples, hoping they could deliver him, but they couldn't."

Jesus said, "What a generation! No sense of God! How many times do I have to go over these things? How much longer do I have to put up with this? Bring the boy here." They brought him. When the demon saw Jesus, it threw the boy into a seizure, causing him to writhe on the ground and foam at the mouth.

He asked the boy's father, "How long has this been going on?"

"Ever since he was a little boy. Many times it pitches him into fire or the river to do away with him. If you can do anything, do it. Have a heart and help us!"

Jesus said, "If? There are no 'ifs' among believers. Anything can happen."

No sooner were the words out of his mouth than the father cried, "Then I believe. Help me with my doubts!"

Seeing that the crowd was forming fast, Jesus gave the vile spirit its marching orders: "Dumb and deaf spirit, I command you—Out of him, and stay out!" Screaming, and with much thrashing about, it left. The boy was pale as a corpse, so people started saying, "He's dead."

But Jesus, taking his hand, raised him. The boy stood up.

Mark 9:14-27 *THE MESSAGE*

Reflect and Respond

As our lives change and the years come and go, we will experience losses, whether small or life changing. Sometimes these losses can really throw us for a loop, making us question our faith and even the goodness and sovereignty of God.

You aren't the first, and you certainly won't be the last, to struggle with trusting God. Though we as believers have the Holy Spirit in our lives to guide and comfort us, we often believe the lies and untruths that God is not enough. Like Anna, we begin to believe that we are on this journey alone. And so we doubt and we wonder and we struggle to believe that God is enough to heal us and make us whole.

Today's Scripture from Mark 9 tells the story of a father who was struggling to believe. This father, dismayed and desperate, came to Jesus for help. We don't know exactly what the man had heard about Jesus' teachings and power, but he most certainly believed that Jesus was an important man and that he had some ability to heal. The man said to Jesus, "If you can do anything, do it." *If.* A small word filled with doubt and uncertainty yet full of hope.

Have you come to Jesus with your own *if*—full of hope but doubting nonetheless? In what ways have you struggled to believe that He can heal you or your situation?

Through Jesus' death on the cross we have been forgiven and made right-eous. Though we may struggle and doubt, God's forgiveness has already been done for us.

How would you define your need for "healing"? What are your expectations for being healed—emotionally, relationally, spiritually, or physically?

The father was struggling, full of doubt and fear, and Jesus called him to believe. Then the father spoke one of the purest prayers ever recorded: *"I believe. Help me with my doubts!"* This simple prayer from a helpless sinner is an acknowledgment that everything comes from God—even faith itself—and that God is the only one who can conquer our doubts and fear and help us believe His promises.

God isn't afraid of our questions and fears. God is big enough to handle them all. In fact, God is so committed to our healing and salvation that He sent his Son, Jesus, to earth. Jesus said, "Healthy people don't need a doctor, but sick people do. Go and learn what this means: I want mercy and not sacrifice. I didn't come to call righteous people, but sinners" (Matthew 9:12-13).

Jesus came for you—despite all of your sin and doubt and self-reliance; despite your inability to trust and to receive. Jesus came to make you whole. And He is able to do just that.

Why is the father's prayer—*"I believe. Help me with my doubts!"*—such a powerful prayer?

Read Isaiah 53:4-5. What does this passage say about Jesus' commitment to heal us and make us whole?

Verse 5 says, "He bore the punishment that made us whole; by his wounds we are healed." All of the verbs in this verse are in the past tense, indicating that this is something that has already been done, that is finished. Through Jesus' death on the cross we have been forgiven and made righteous. Though we may struggle and doubt, God's forgiveness has already been done for us.

Why, then, do you think we often struggle with doubt?

Read 2 Corinthians 12:9. Do you believe that God's grace is enough for you? How might truly believing this affect your daily life?

Read Luke 11:9. How does this verse encourage you to trust God and God's healing work in your life?

Talk to God

Dear God, I want to know you more, to trust in your love and goodness. God, help my doubts and my unbelief. Help me, each day, to put down my fears and my doubts and to pick up your love and faithfulness. Remind me that because of your amazing gift of salvation through Jesus, I am free to experience the kind of healing in my heart that only you can provide. Amen.

As You Go

Consider the father's prayer: *"I believe. Help me with my doubts!"* About what area(s) of your life can you pray this prayer today?

DAY 4: HELP ALONG THE JOURNEY

As we continue on this journey to healing, we no doubt need help and support along the way. In the coming weeks, we will explore how God has equipped us for this journey and how God sends others to walk alongside us to support us and enrich our lives. What we'll find is that God gives us exactly what we need, when we need it.

Read God's Word

But Moses said to the LORD, "My LORD, I've never been able to speak well, not yesterday, not the day before, and certainly not now since you've been talking to your servant. I have a slow mouth and a thick tongue."

Then the LORD said to him, "Who gives people the ability to speak? Who's responsible for making them unable to speak or hard of hearing, sighted or blind? Isn't it I, the LORD? Now go! I'll help you speak, and I'll teach you what you should say."

But Moses said, "Please, my LORD, just send someone else."

Then the LORD got angry at Moses and said, "What about your brother Aaron the Levite? I know he can speak very well. He's on his way out to meet you now, and he's looking forward to seeing you. Speak to him and tell him what he's supposed to say. I'll help both of you speak, and I'll teach both of you what to do. Aaron will speak for you to the people. He'll be a spokesperson for you, and you will be like God for him.

Exodus 4:10-16

Reflect and Respond

God has plans for your life, just as God had plans for Moses' life. God created you for good things. And what God has created you for, God will equip you to accomplish. If you have your doubts, just read Ephesians 2:10: "We are God's accomplishment, created in Christ Jesus to do good things. God planned for these good things to be the way that we live our lives." God will give us the strength and faith we need for the journey ahead and will be with us every step of the way, just as he was with Moses.

Of course, Moses had his doubts at first. When God shared his big plans for Moses to be the instrument that would lead the Jewish people out of enslavement in Egypt, Moses was timid and afraid that he was not capable of what God was asking him to do.

What were Moses' fears, and how did God respond?

> God has plans for your life, just as God had plans for Moses' life. God created you for good things. And what God has created you for, God will equip you to accomplish.

Has there ever been a time in your life when you felt incapable of doing something that God called you to do? If so, what was the situation, and what was the outcome? What did you learn from the experience?

The good news is that God listens to us. God understands our insecurities and fears and knows that sometimes we need others in our lives to help us along the way. Moses was afraid to speak, and so God gave him a helper with a voice—his brother Aaron.

Mark 2 tells a beautiful story of the role that faithful friendship played in one man's life:

After a few days, Jesus went back to Capernaum, and people heard that he was at home. So many gathered that there was no longer space, not even near the door. Jesus was speaking the word to them. Some people arrived, and four of them were bringing to him a man who was paralyzed. They couldn't carry him through the crowd, so they tore off part of the roof above where Jesus was. When they had made an opening, they lowered the mat on which the paralyzed man was lying. When Jesus saw their faith, he said to the paralytic, "Child, your sins are forgiven! . . . Get up, take your mat, and go home." Jesus raised him up, and right away he picked up his mat and walked out in front of everybody. They were all amazed and praised God, saying, "We've never seen anything like this!"

Mark 2:1-5, 11-12

Galatians 6:2 says, "Carry each other's burdens and so you will fulfill the law of Christ." Those four men literally carried their bedridden friend to where Jesus was, and when they ran into obstacles and hardship, they did not give up. They fought for their friend's healing, and Jesus honored their faith and determination.

We need other believers in our lives to fight for us—to pray for us, to speak truth to us, to walk with us.

Read 1 Thessalonians 5:11-22. What are some ways we are told to live in community with other believers?

Read Colossians 3:15-16. In *The Message* paraphrase, Paul admonishes these early believers to "let the peace of Christ keep you in tune with each other, in

> We need other believers in our lives to fight for us—to pray for us, to speak truth to us, to walk with us.

step with each other. None of this going off and doing your own thing." Why do you think Paul gives this instruction?

Why is it important for us to walk in community with other believers?

Who has God put in your life to walk with you these next several weeks as you explore healing in your life? What kind of help and support can you ask for from them?

Oftentimes physical places can be conduits for our healing—places where we can go to experience peace and calm, and to dream and hope for new beginnings.

A true blessing in Anna's life was Hazel, a woman of strength and confidence who walked with Anna and helped her realize new dreams for her life.

Excerpt from *River's Song,* Chapter 11

[Hazel said to Anna,] *"You treat me too well and I will never want to leave this place."* Hazel got a thoughtful look. *"You know this location would be a wonderful spot for an inn. Have you ever considered that? After the lumber people move on—and I suspect they will—it will be up to people like you to help the land and the river to heal again."*

"To heal again—" Anna rolled those words around in her mind. *"I like the sound of that."*

Hazel smiled. *"I suspect you have a healer inside of you."*

"What do you mean?"

She waved her hand over the cabin. *"You took something that was ailing and in need of help . . . and you made it better. You, my dear, are a healer."*

Anna felt a rush of pride and wonder. *"I hope that's true. I usually think of the river as having the power to heal me. Maybe I could help it to heal too."*

· · · · · · ·

In addition to people, sometimes God uses places to help us along our journeys. In The Inn at Shining Waters Series, the river is a place of healing for Anna, and it becomes the impetus for Anna's hope and dream to create an inn that will be a place of hope and healing for many people. The natural beauty of the river and the remote location seem to lend a sense of calm, serenity, and groundedness to the lives of those who come there.

Often physical places can be conduits for our healing—places where we can go to experience peace and calm, and to dream and hope for new beginnings. Like Anna, for many of us being surrounded by nature can give us a renewed sense of joy and purpose, while others are most inspired by the majesty of a beautiful cathedral or the comfort of a quiet, cozy corner in which to meditate.

What physical places restore and revive your spirit? What places and spaces move you?

Read Psalm 19:1. How can beauty—especially the beauty that is found in nature—encourage and comfort us? Why do you think we are so affected by and connected to nature?

Read Psalm 122:1. Do you relate to the psalmist's joy? Why or why not?

During this journey to discover healing, what places can you go to for refuge and encouragement? Is there somewhere you can regularly go for peace and calm and meditation?

Talk to God

Lord God, I know that I am not on this journey alone. You have called me onto this path of healing, and I know that you will provide everything I need along the way. Thank you for so faithfully looking after me and caring about my needs. I want to know you more, God. I want to know your love and healing and grace. Open my eyes to see you; open my ears to hear you. Amen.

As You Go

As you spend time in God's Word through this study over the next several weeks, consider what you need to make the most of each lesson. Do you need to reserve a space in your home where you can focus and meditate peacefully? Will you need to enlist others to help you protect this space and time? Today, plan how you can make the most of this study.

DAY 5: LET MY WHOLE BEING BLESS THE LORD

The text of Psalm 103 will be our foundational Scripture throughout this study. This psalm, written by David, speaks to God's just, holy, and loving nature and proclaims the love, care, goodness, and healing that God extends to us on a daily basis. In the remaining weeks, we will consider how the text of this psalm relates to the stories of healing in The Inn at Shining Waters Series, as well as to your own journey of healing.

Read God's Word

Read through the following psalm several times, reading it aloud at least once. Circle or underline phrases and words that speak directly to your heart. Meditate on the passage and pray the words of the text.

> *1 Let my whole being bless the LORD!*
> *Let everything inside me*
> *bless his holy name!*
> *2 Let my whole being bless the LORD*
> *and never forget all his good deeds:*
> *3 how God forgives all your sins,*
> *heals all your sickness,*
> *4 saves your life from the pit,*
> *crowns you with faithful love*
> *and compassion,*

5 and satisfies you
with plenty of good things
so that your youth
is made fresh like an eagle's.
6 The LORD works righteousness;
does justice for all who are oppressed.
7 God made his ways known to Moses;
made his deeds known
to the Israelites.
8 The LORD is compassionate
and merciful,
very patient, and full of faithful love.
9 God won't always play the judge;
he won't be angry forever.
10 He doesn't deal with us
according to our sin
or repay us
according to our wrongdoing,
11 because as high as heaven
is above the earth,
that's how large God's faithful love
is for those who honor him.
12 As far as east is from west—
that's how far God has removed
our sin from us.
13 Like a parent feels compassion
for their children—
that's how the LORD feels compassion for those who honor him.
14 Because God knows how we're made,
God remembers we're just dust.
15 The days of a human life are like grass:
they bloom like a wildflower;
16 but when the wind blows through it,
it's gone;
even the ground where it stood
doesn't remember it.
17 But the LORD's faithful love is from forever ago to forever from now
for those who honor him.
And God's righteousness reaches
to the grandchildren
18 of those who keep his covenant
and remember to keep his commands.

19 The LORD has established his throne
in heaven,
and his kingdom rules over all.
20 You divine messengers,
bless the LORD!
You who are mighty in power
and keep his word,
who obey everything he says,
bless him!
21 All you heavenly forces,
bless the LORD!
All you who serve him and do his will,
bless him!
22 All God's creatures,
bless the LORD!
Everywhere, throughout his kingdom,
let my whole being
bless the LORD!
Psalm 103

Reflect and Respond

The first half of David's psalm (verses 1-14) is devoted to praise for God's mercy and miraculous gift of salvation to us—sinners who desperately need mercy. Verses 9-11 proclaim that God does not deal with us as we deserve but loves us faithfully beyond measure.

Read John 3:16-17. How do these verses speak to the fact that God "doesn't deal with us according to our sin or repay us according to our wrongdoing"?

Read Zephaniah 3:17. How does it make you feel to know that God is fighting for you?

Read Psalm 103:3-5 again, circling the verbs that describe what God is doing for you. Which one is most meaningful to you today, and why?

The second half of the psalm (verses 15-22) proclaims God's consistent faithfulness and His power and authority. Though our lives are short and filled with uncertainty, we can trust in God because God does not change. The Lord, infinite and strong, watches over the days of our lives, covering us with mercy and goodness. God was there when the earth began and will continue long after we are gone. Therefore we can trust God with our lives.

What does Jeremiah 10:12 say about God's power and authority?

> Though our lives are short and filled with uncertainty, we can trust in God because God does not change. The Lord, infinite and strong, watches over the days of our lives, covering us with mercy and goodness.

Anna would never have dreamed that the previous years of her life had been preparing her for a life of fulfillment and happiness. She was pleasantly surprised to find, however, that the years of taking care of Eunice and Lauren and their household were paving the way for her natural gifts of hospitality to shine through.

Excerpt from *River's Song,* Chapter 16

After the meal was finished, Clark politely thanked Anna, complimenting her again on her fine cooking abilities. It was pleasant to hear his praise, but as she cleaned up the breakfast things, she wondered if he saw her beyond a good cook and housekeeper. Oh, she knew that fairly adequately described her life. Certainly that's what her mother-in-law had trained her to be. In fact, it seemed that Eunice had spent the past two decades trying to obliterate Anna's spirit by reducing her to the role of domestic servant.

As she scrubbed a dish, just like she'd done thousands of times before, Anna could relate to James Dean's Rebel Without a Cause, *except that Anna thought she had a cause worthy of rebelling against. After all, didn't she deserve a life beyond cooking and cleaning? What was she getting herself into with her dreams to run an inn? Wasn't that just like signing up for more of the same . . . or worse? What if she was, like Daddy used to say, jumping from the frying pan into the fire?*

Yet strangely, as she took her time to clean up and put things away, she found a sense of solace and comfort in doing these familiar everyday things. Was it that she actually enjoyed menial tasks? Or perhaps her pleasure came from knowing she was not doing this service for her mother-in-law—who could never be pleased—but for herself. Not only that, but she could do these things when and how she liked—or not at all if she so chose. And it was her business if she decided to do these tasks for others. As long as she was happy and content like she felt now while drying a platter and looking out over the sparkling river, why should she doubt herself? Why not simply enjoy it?

• • • • • • •

Consider this question: Do you believe God's power is at work in your life? How does the way you live your life reflect the answer to this question?

Talk to God

Lord God, I praise you for your faithful love for me. Help me to trust you completely with my life. I believe that you are walking this journey with me, God, and that you will be with me on my journey to healing. May my whole being bless you! Amen.

As You Go

Choose a verse or short passage from Psalm 103 to meditate on throughout the day. Pray that God's words will penetrate your heart. Journal your thoughts about this passage—or the entire psalm—and how it speaks to you (journaling pages are provided at the back of the book).

VIDEO NOTES
A FEW MINUTES WITH MELODY

INTERESTING INSIGHTS:

POINTS I'D LIKE TO DISCUSS WITH THE GROUP:

WEEK 2
DISCOVERING FORGIVENESS

Scripture for the Week

*Let my whole being bless the L*ORD
and never forget all his good deeds:
how God forgives all your sins,
heals all your sickness,
saves your life from the pit,
crowns you with faithful love
and compassion,
and satisfies you
with plenty of good things
so that your youth
is made fresh like an eagle's.
Psalm 103:2–5

Excerpt from *River's Song*, Chapter 24

[A]*nna's] mother loved violets—everything about them, their velvety petals, the rich color of purple, but most of all the smell. And that reminded Anna of one of her mother's favorite sayings.*

"Forgiveness is the sweet fragrance of violets on the heel that crushed them,"
Mother would sometimes say with a twinkle in her eye as she arranged the delicate blooms in the tiny vase. But Anna had never quite understood the meaning of this saying. Her thinking was that no one should go around trampling on violets—especially not on purpose—and certainly not in order to walk around with sweet smelling shoes. That was wasteful and wrong.

But she considered it now. Forgiveness . . . like the smell of crushed violets . . . on the feet that trampled over them. [Anna] felt that [her mother-in-law], Eunice, had trampled over her—many a time. . . . Did that mean Anna needed to release something that smelled as sweet as violets to Eunice? Never mind that Eunice didn't deserve such a gift. But how was that even possible? Was Anna supposed to send Eunice some perfume?

Anna sat the vase in the center of the table and just stared at its sparkling cut surface as it reflected the light. Just like that, Anna understood perfectly. She needed to

39

forgive Eunice—whether or not Eunice deserved it. And Anna realized that when she forgave Eunice, it would be like releasing the sweet smell of violets on the heel that had crushed her. Simple enough…just not easy. Once again, she prayed, asking for God's help—and believing that he could show her how to forgive someone who had walked all over her [for many, many years].

Anna awoke feeling refreshed and at peace the next morning. She was still sad that [her daughter], Lauren, wouldn't be coming to visit [her at the river], but she felt hopeful that someday—maybe not too far in the future—Lauren would come. With breakfast preparations already in process, Anna slipped outside and went around to the shady corner where Mother's little patch of violets used to grow. Slightly overgrown with grass and weeds, Anna pushed it back to see that there were still some violets growing there. She picked a tiny bouquet then went back into the house to put it in the tiny vase.

She was just stirring huckleberries into the pancake batter when she heard someone come in. "Good morning," she called out cheerfully.

"Good morning," Clark said gently. "How are you feeling this morning?"

"Quite well." She smiled brightly.

"Oh, that's good to know. I was worried that you'd taken Joe Miller's news a lot harder than I'd expected you would."

She waved her hand. "No, no. I wasn't upset over that. Well, perhaps a tiny bit, but no, that's not what was troubling me last night." Now she confided to him about her disturbing conversation with Lauren, [wherein her daughter accused her of trying to tear the family apart]. "It was hard enough to hear she's not coming today. But to find out that she thinks I'm robbing Eunice of everything…well, that was difficult."

"It sounds as if Eunice is poisoning your daughter's mind."

Anna pressed her lips together, wondering how she could make him understand.

"Perhaps I should send Eunice a legal letter, warning her that she needs—"

"No," Anna said quickly. "Please, don't do that." Now she walked over to where the vase of violets was in the center of the dining room table and she explained to him about her mother's saying.

"I think I've heard that before." Still, he looked a bit bewildered.

"So I have decided to forgive Eunice," she said as she walked back to the kitchen. "Even though Eunice doesn't deserve to be forgiven, just like the heel doesn't deserve to smell sweet, I will give it to her." She stopped at the big new stove, turning on the flame without having to strike a match.

Clark nodded with a thoughtful expression. "I respect that. In fact, I think it's not only very mature of you, but it's very wise as well."

"Wise?" She tipped her head to one side.

"I've learned, from experience, that when you withhold forgiveness from someone it puts you into a kind of bondage with them. It's like they own a piece of your soul if you remain bitter." He sighed. "I did that with Roselyn, [my ex-wife], for a number of years before I figured it out."

"So you've forgiven her?"

He grinned. "The truth is it's kind of a process with me. I find I have to forgive her again and again. But hopefully in time I'll get beyond it altogether."

Anna smiled. "I think it might be like that for me with Eunice too."

• • • • • • •

DAY 1: THE BIRTH OF FORGIVENESS

Read God's Word

The woman saw that the tree was beautiful with delicious food and that the tree would provide wisdom, so she took some of its fruit and ate it, and also gave some to her husband, who was with her, and he ate it. Then they both saw clearly and knew that they were naked. So they sewed fig leaves together and made garments for themselves.

During that day's cool evening breeze, they heard the sound of the LORD God walking in the garden; and the man and his wife hid themselves from the LORD God in the middle of the garden's trees.

Genesis 3:6-8

Reflect and Respond

It didn't take long for humanity to fail. Despite being loved, cared for, and in fellowship with their Creator, Adam and Eve allowed doubt to gain a foothold in their lives, and, in one tantalizing bite, betrayed the One who promised them every good thing. Sin entered the world, and the pure fellowship that they had enjoyed with God was broken.

Though it was a rocky beginning, thus began the beautiful story of God's pursuit of humankind and His plan for the redemption of our souls. Just as sin was birthed into the world, God's divine plan was set in motion to bring forgiveness to all of God's people, to restore that relationship which was lost, and to make things right in the way only God can.

God's plan was to send His Son, Jesus, to Earth, to become a human and live among His people. Though Jesus would be a man, He would be a sinless man, a feat un-attainable for mere mortals. He would speak of the goodness and love of God and declare God's plan for the redemption of the people's sins. Jesus declared, "I am the way, the truth, and the life. No one comes to the Father except through me" (John 14:6). He would be abused and ridiculed by the self-righteous and the fearful, and then He would be sacrificed, the weight of humanity's sins on His shoulders. God's justice would be satisfied through His blood. Our sins would be paid for, forgiven once and for all, in this one miraculous event.

When it was done, the earth rose and shuddered, as if taking a cleansing breath. The broken relationship was restored. It was done, and it was good.

Read John 3:19–20. When have you felt ashamed about something you did or said? Were you eager to confess it and get it off your chest, or did you want to hide it and keep others from knowing about it?

Jesus' sacrifice allows us to receive God's forgiveness, and that forgiveness is so complete that the Bible says, "As far as east is from west—that's how far God has removed our sin from us" (Psalm 103:12).

Reread Genesis 3:6–8. What do these verses say about how Adam and Eve reacted after they betrayed God?

Have you ever had this experience—when a sinful action opened your eyes and caused you to become more aware of yourself and your sin? What did you do with that knowledge? Did it cause you to run from God or to God?

Romans 3:23 says, "All have sinned and fall short of God's glory." All of us—every human being on earth—have made mistakes and sinned against our God and those we love. But there is good news. Verse 24 continues, "But all are treated as righteous freely by his grace because of a ransom that was paid by Christ Jesus."

Jesus' sacrifice allows us to receive God's forgiveness, and that forgiveness is so complete that the Bible says, "As far as east is from west—that's how far God has removed our sin from us" (Psalm 103:12).

It's not just that God forgives and forgets; when God looks at us through the sacrifice of his Son, it's as if we never sinned in the first place. What an amazing gift!

Have you ever received a gift that you felt you didn't deserve? How did you react to that gift?

Have you accepted God's offer of forgiveness? If so, how has that gift changed your life?

How does it make you feel to hear the words of Psalm 103:12: "As far as east is from west—that's how far God has removed our sin from us"? Do you feel freed from your sins? If not, why do you think that's so?

What does 2 Corinthians 5:17 have to say about our status as believers?

How does this week's Scripture focus, Psalm 103:2-5, encourage you today?

Talk to God

Heavenly Father, thank you for the gift of forgiveness—the gift of salvation— through your Son, Jesus Christ. Help me to remember what you've done for me, and that I am free from the bonds of sin and shame. Amen.

As You Go

Read and reflect on the message of these verses today:

> *God's righteousness comes through the faithfulness of Jesus Christ for all who have faith in him. There's no distinction. All have sinned and fall short of God's glory, but all are treated as righteous freely by his grace because of a ransom that was paid by Christ Jesus. Through his faithfulness, God displayed Jesus as the place of sacrifice where mercy is found by means of his blood. He did this to demonstrate his righteousness in passing over sins that happened before, during the time of God's patient tolerance. He also did this to demonstrate that he is righteous in the present time, and to treat the one who has faith in Jesus as righteous.*
> Romans 3:22–26

DAY 2: ACCEPTING FORGIVENESS

To hear about the gracious, extravagant love of God is one thing; to accept it and embrace it as part of our lives is another. It often seems too good to be true, doesn't it? That God would offer us a perfect, unconditional gift, not based on our merit or performance but bestowed on us when we couldn't help ourselves, is amazing.

The Gospel of John tells of many miracles that Jesus performed when He walked on Earth, and many lives that He touched with His human hands. It was on one of those days that Jesus changed the life of one man who was waiting for something good to happen to him.

Read God's Word

After this there was a Jewish festival, and Jesus went up to Jerusalem. In Jerusalem near the Sheep Gate in the north city wall is a pool with the Aramaic name Bethsaida. It had five covered porches, and a crowd of people who were sick, blind, lame, and paralyzed sat there. A certain man was there who had been sick for thirty-eight years. When Jesus saw him lying there, knowing that he had already been there a long time, he asked him, "Do you want to get well?"

The sick man answered him, "Sir, I don't have anyone who can put me in the water when it is stirred up. When I'm trying to get to it, someone else has gotten in ahead of me."

Jesus said to him, "Get up! Pick up your mat and walk." Immediately the man was well, and he picked up his mat and walked.

John 5:1–9

Reflect and Respond

It was time for the Jewish festival of Passover, and Jesus had gone to Jerusalem to celebrate and observe the holy event. The city was no doubt crowded with throngs of people making the annual trip, and the pool at Bethsaida was especially crowded—brimming with those who were sick, blind, and paralyzed. They all waited near the pool in great anticipation, for it was known to be a miraculous place of healing. From time to time, an angel would come and stir the waters of the pool, and whoever was the first to step into the pool would be cured and made whole. So the people came, and they waited.

As Jesus walked among the despondent crowd, he saw him. One man, probably older than most, was waiting. Scripture says that he had been sick for thirty-eight years, longer than the whole life span of many in this day and age. Who knows how long he had been waiting at the pool, waiting for a miracle. Maybe he was hopeful every day that he would be healed; perhaps he had given up long ago but didn't have anywhere else to go. Regardless, Jesus asked him a question: "Do you want to get well?"

> That God would offer us a perfect, unconditional gift, not based on our merit or performance but bestowed on us when we couldn't help ourselves, is amazing.

This seems a strange question to ask someone who had been defined by his disability for so many years. Wouldn't the obvious answer be "yes"? Why do you think Jesus asked this question?

Note that the man's answer is not a resounding, "Yes!" Instead he says, "Sir, I don't have anyone who can put me in the water when it is stirred up. When I'm trying to get to it, someone else has gotten in ahead of me" (v.7).

What do you hear in the man's answer? Anger? Frustration? Resignation? How do you picture him responding to Jesus?

When we are able to wholeheartedly accept Christ's redemption and free grace given to us, we receive a strength we never believed possible.

The question seems odd, but this question from Jesus probes at our hearts, asking, "Will you accept the gift I've given you? Do you want to be freed from your sin? Are you willing to let me make you whole? Are you willing to be healed?"

Do you believe that Jesus sees you—really sees you—all of your hopes, desires, failings, longings, and doubts?

How does it make you feel to know you've been pursued, singled out by God?

"Jesus said to him, 'Get up! Pick up your mat and walk.' Immediately the man was well, and he picked up his mat and walked" (vv. 8–9). The man left behind what had been and embraced what he had received. Now he was free—free to believe that his life could be different, that he now had something to give.

When we are able to wholeheartedly accept Christ's redemption and free grace given to us, we receive a strength we never believed possible. We are free to be generous and lavish others with forgiveness, knowing that God is the one in charge. Like Anna found the strength to accept her own failings and weaknesses and then was moved to forgive Eunice, we can find the strength to offer forgiveness to others, even when they don't ask for it.

How does this passage speak to you? Do you identify with the man at the pool? How? How is Jesus calling you into healing?

Talk to God

Jesus, thank you for your extravagant gift of grace. You offer it so freely and with such power and authority. Help me to fully accept your gift. Help me to know that you see me—that you know where I need to be healed and forgiven, and that your words have the power to transform my life. Amen.

As You Go

In what areas of your life do you have trouble believing that you are forgiven? Confess those areas to God today and ask for God's peace and reassurance.

> The choice to continue to love another is often a deliberate one, a commitment to actively love, even when it's not easy or convenient. In the same way, forgiveness is a choice.

DAY 3: EMBRACING FORGIVENESS

Read God's Word

Make sure that no one misses out on God's grace. Make sure that no root of bitterness grows up that might cause trouble and pollute many people.

Hebrews 12:15

Reflect and Respond

It has often been said that love is a choice, not a feeling. Though romantic, emotional feelings of love can sometimes be fickle, the choice to continue to love another is often a deliberate one, a commitment to actively love, even when it's not easy or convenient.

In the same way, forgiveness is a choice. When we are hurt and betrayed by someone, it's not likely that we'll be excited and eager to extend grace and forgiveness. Instead, it's more likely that we will have to make a conscious, deliberate choice to begin the hard, healing process of forgiveness. As today's Scripture says, we must "make sure"

THEME 1: *RIVER'S SONG*

to extend God's grace and forgiveness through a conscious choice of our will. This choice prevents a root of bitterness from springing up within our hearts and souls.

For years Anna endured her mother-in-law's harsh criticism, put-downs, and insults, all while living under Eunice's roof and taking care of her household. When Anna thinks about how Eunice, her mother-in-law, has treated her over the years, how do you think it makes Anna feel? How do you think that relationship has affected Anna's life?

Recognizing the wisdom found in Grandma Pearl's ancient stories, Hazel encourages Anna on her journey of forgiveness and healing with a story Grandma Pearl once told.

Excerpt from *River's Song,* Chapter 14

[Hazel] cleared her throat, looking straight ahead as she held on to the steering wheel with both hands, turning onto the graveled road. "Long, long ago in the cave by the beach there lived a fearsome cave monster. He was big and hairy with long sharp teeth and claws. Every living thing within miles feared this cave monster, and naturally, the horrible cave monster only came out at night."

"Naturally." Anna smiled at how Hazel always put her own little touches on these stories. Perhaps that was what Grandma had done too. Maybe everyone did that in their own way.

"But when the monster came out at night, he always killed and destroyed and devoured anything in his path, wiping out seals and sea lions and beaver and otters— he'd tear them to pieces then eat them whole, flesh and hair and bone, nothing left. No living creature was safe when the cave monster roamed at night."

"No wonder Grandma didn't tell me this story, I probably would've had terrible nightmares."

"So one day the chief of the sea lions decided he'd had enough of the cave monster. He wanted to get rid of him once and for all. But he wasn't sure how to do it. So the chief of the sea lions went to see Old Otter, because everyone knew, Old Otter was very wise. The chief of sea lions asked Otter how they could get rid of the cave monster."

"And?" Anna waited.

"Old Otter told the sea lion chief to gather up all the seaweed in the sea and to have his sea lions braid them together to make a long, long rope. Then he said to tie this rope to the biggest spear they had and to throw it at the sun. Then, when it hit the sun, they were to all pull together to haul down the sun and hide it so that daytime looked like night."

"Was the chief sea lion able to do this?"

"Yes. He did as Otter said and pulled down the sun and hid it. Naturally, the cave monster thought it was nighttime, so he emerged from his cave and was about to start slaughtering everything he could find—but just then the sea lions released their hold on the sun and it shot back into the sky so it was light and bright and daytime again."

"And?" Anna was actually curious now.

"And the brightness of the sun caused the cave monster to go completely blind and as he tried to stumble back to his cave, the sea lion chief picked up the spear he'd used on the sun and killed the cave monster so that he could never wreak havoc among them again."

Anna clapped her hands. "Good! Because that cave monster sounded like a really nasty fellow."

Hazel nodded. "Isn't it interesting how the fear of darkness translates across all cultures? It doesn't matter what part of the earth one is from, that thing that goes bump in the night scares everyone."

"Perhaps because there have always been real dangers at night," Anna said. "There still are in some places today. Even on the river there are cougars, bears, bobcats—they all feed at night—and you don't really want to come up on one unawares."

> "Sometimes we are most afraid of what we don't know—what we can't see or hear or understand unsettles us."

"That's true enough. But I suppose I was wondering more about the metaphor in general. Darkness can symbolize ignorance, a lack of enlightenment, and sometimes we are most afraid of what we don't know—what we can't see or hear or understand unsettles us. In the darkest hours of our ignorance, our imaginations and fears can run amok. Whereas, we don't usually feel the same way in the clarity of daytime—or when we're fully aware of what's going on. Fear and misunderstanding are bred in the absence of enlightenment."

"So those people, the ones who live in ignorance of their fellow man, are not unlike the cave monster," Anna mused. "If they choose to live in darkness, they set themselves up to become destructive."

• • • • • • •

How can living in the darkness of unforgiveness be destructive?

Reread today's Scripture, Hebrews 12:15. How does this verse speak to the need to forgive others?

Anna decides to forgive Eunice. Based on what you know about Eunice and her stubborn pride, how do you think she will react to and accept Anna's forgiveness?

Just as refusing to forgive others is self-destructive to our own lives, how can refusing to accept another's forgiveness be just as damaging?

Talk to God

Lord, do not allow the bitter root of unforgiveness to sprout in my heart. Reveal to me where I am unbending and stubborn, and to whom I need to extend grace and forgiveness. Open my eyes to my hurts and long-held grudges, and help me to release those today. Amen.

As You Go

Reflect and meditate on this passage from the Lord's Prayer: "Forgive us for the ways we have wronged you, just as we also forgive those who have wronged us" (Matthew 6:12). How is God calling you to respond?

Day 4: Forgiveness Is a Process

Read God's Word

Then Peter said to Jesus, "Lᴏʀᴅ, how many times should I forgive my brother or sister who sins against me? Should I forgive as many as seven times?"

Jesus said, "Not just seven times, but rather as many as seventy-seven times. Therefore the kingdom of heaven is like a king who wanted to settle accounts with his servants. When he began to settle accounts, they brought to him a servant who owed him ten thousand bags of gold. Because the servant didn't have enough to pay it back, the master ordered that he should be sold, along with his wife and children and everything he had, and that the proceeds should be used as payment. But the servant fell down, kneeled before him, and said, 'Please, be patient with me, and I'll pay you back.' The master had compassion on that servant, released him, and forgave the loan.

"When that servant went out, he found one of his fellow servants who owed him one hundred coins. He grabbed him around the throat and said, 'Pay me back what you owe me.'

"Then his fellow servant fell down and begged him, 'Be patient with me, and I'll pay you back.' But he refused. Instead, he threw him into prison until he paid back his debt.

"When his fellow servants saw what happened, they were deeply offended. They came and told their master all that happened. His master called the first servant and said, 'You wicked servant! I forgave you all that debt because you appealed to me. Shouldn't you also have mercy on your fellow servant, just as I had mercy on you?' His master was furious and handed him over to the guard responsible for punishing prisoners, until he had paid the whole debt.

"My heavenly Father will also do the same to you if you don't forgive your brother or sister from your heart."

Matthew 18:21–35

Reflect and Respond

The dictionary defines the action of forgiving as "to cease to feel resentment against an offender" and "to give up resentment of or claim to compensation or retaliation." When someone hurts us, many emotions and reactions spring to life. We are hurt, devastated, angry; we want justice and punishment for the wrongs committed.

What is your typical response when someone hurts or offends you? Do you retaliate verbally? Do you shut down and internalize the hurt? How do you react?

Do you find it easy to forgive, or do you tend to hold on to offenses?

Because we have been so fully and graciously forgiven by God, God calls us to forgive others generously and completely. But when the hurt is deep, offering that kind of forgiveness to others can seem virtually impossible.

It's important to realize that forgiveness is a process, one that often doesn't come quickly and easily. It is making a choice to continually offer up our hurt and disappointment to our Creator and asking Him to help us forgive, over and over again.

Although my own mother-in-law was nothing like the despicable Eunice, she was what I would call the "difficult person" in my life. I wouldn't be surprised if I had to forgive her "seventy-seven times" during the nearly three decades that I knew her, but I believed that as a Christian it was my responsibility to do so. It took me years to understand that many of her "difficulties" were related to a very dysfunctional childhood, as well as being part Cherokee in a predominantly "white" community. In the final years before her death, she shared some of her heartbreaking memories with me…and we cried together. Although it was hard to do at times and I always needed God's help, I'm so thankful I chose to forgive her.

Forgiveness is a process. Perhaps that's why Jesus says we are to forgive "seventy-seven times." When old hurts and resentments surface, we need to come to Him again and again, perhaps day after day, asking for the strength to forgive and let go.

We're all familiar with the commonly used phrase "forgive and forget." Do you believe that something is only forgiven if it's forgotten? Why or why not?

How have you experienced forgiveness as a process in your own life?

Soon after Anna decides to forgive Eunice, Anna's childhood friend Dorothy comes home to visit and stops by to see Anna. Excited to reunite with her old friend, Anna invites Dorothy and her two daughters, Jill and Joanna, to stay with her at the lake house.

> It's important to realize that forgiveness is a process, one that often doesn't come quickly and easily. It is making a choice to continually offer up our hurt and disappointment to our Creator and asking Him to help us forgive, over and over again.

51

Excerpt from *River's Song,* Chapter 25

The next few days passed far too quickly. Anna loved hosting her friend and the girls. They did all the things she'd hoped to do with Lauren and her friends—boating, swimming, fishing and lighting campfires—but on the last night there, after the girls had gone to bed, Dorothy confessed to Anna that her marriage was in serious trouble. She had discovered that her husband had been involved with another woman. "I'm just devastated," she said sadly. "I don't know what I'm going to do—to stay or to go. Either option feels hopeless to me. I came out here hoping to figure things out."

Anna didn't know what to say.

"I'd leave him, but I can't imagine being on my own at my age." Dorothy frowned and shook her head. "I don't have any job skills or source of income. I feel so helpless, and hurt, and then I get angry."

"Do you still love him?"

Dorothy's mouth twisted to one side. "I shouldn't. But I suppose I do."

"Do you think he still loves you?"

"He says he does."

"Do you think you can ever forgive him?"

Dorothy held up her hands. "I don't know. He swears he'll never do it again—but how can I be sure?"

Now Anna told her about her mother-in-law and then she explained about the violets and how it wasn't easy, but how she was trying to forgive Eunice. "It's like a friend of mine told me, forgiveness is a process. But I'm working on it. In fact, I've been thinking about this very thing this past week. Like I mentioned, I want this inn to be special, a place of healing, and I feel certain that forgiveness has a direct link to healing."

Dorothy slowly nodded. "I sort of understand that. Constantly being angry at Ralph makes my stomach hurt. I honestly think it could be giving me an ulcer. You should see how I go through the Pepto-Bismol."

"I wouldn't be surprised if it was making you ill. Bitterness is like a sickness."

They talked late into the night, and before Dorothy went to bed she decided she was going to attempt to forgive her husband. "I think it's what I really wanted to do all along," she admitted, "but I just didn't think he deserved it. Now I'm going to remember those violets."

· · · · · · ·

[Anna said,] "I want this inn to be special, a place of healing, and I feel certain that forgiveness has a direct link to healing."

Often the desire to forgive someone doesn't come quickly or easily. Have you, like Dorothy, ever had a hard time deciding whether or not to forgive someone? How did you feel during that in-between time?

During her time of pain and searching, Dorothy hears truth and receives comfort from her friend Anna. To whom do you turn when you are hurting and in pain? Where do you go to seek truth in your situation?

Many people say that time heals our wounds. Have you found that to be true in your own life? How so?

Talk to God

Dear God, thank you for gently reminding me that all of life is a work-in-progress, and that you will give me the strength I need to get through each day. Help me to have a forgiving heart and to desire reconciliation and peace in my relationships. Amen.

As You Go

To whom is God asking you to extend forgiveness? Are you hesitating? Ask God for the strength and direction to obey His guidance today.

DAY 5: FREEDOM IN FORGIVENESS

Read God's Word

> *Let my whole being bless the LORD*
> *and never forget all his good deeds:*
> *how God forgives all your sins,*
> *heals all your sickness,*
> *saves your life from the pit,*
> *crowns you with faithful love*
> *and compassion,*
> *and satisfies you*
> *with plenty of good things*
> *so that your youth*
> *is made fresh like an eagle's.*
> Psalm 103:2–5

But whenever someone turns back to the Lord, the veil is removed. The Lord is the Spirit, and where the Lord's Spirit is, there is freedom. All of us are looking with unveiled faces at the glory of the Lord as if we were looking in a mirror. We are being transformed into that same image from one degree of glory to the next degree of glory. This comes from the Lord, who is the Spirit.

2 Corinthians 3:16–18

Youths will become tired and weary, young men will certainly stumble; but those who hope in the LORD will renew their strength; they will fly up on wings like eagles; they will run and not be tired; they will walk and not be weary.

Isaiah 40:30–31

Reflect and Respond

Living in the land of bitterness and unforgiveness can be a dark and lonely place. But when we pray for the strength to forgive, we are asking God to come and shine divine light in the dark places, to bring healing power to the deepest corners of our hearts and release us from the weight and pain of our circumstances. Today's Scripture passages speak freely about the renewing nature of God.

Which Scripture speaks most clearly into your life right now? Why?

Reread the three passages, circling words and phrases that describe renewal and transformation. Which word or phrase is most encouraging to you and why?

Living in the land of bitterness and unforgiveness can be a dark and lonely place. But when we pray for the strength to forgive, we are asking God to come and shine divine light in the dark places. . . .

Our willingness to forgive invites God to give us supernatural strength and provision. Through forgiveness we will be refreshed and renewed with hearts that are blessed through obedience and are free to love and live out God's plan.

When Anna chooses to forgive Eunice, and to act out that forgiveness, she feels a freedom that she didn't know was possible. What might that forgiveness free her to do, both emotionally and practically?

Why do you think forgiveness and obedience lift weights off of our hearts?

Does it always feel great to be obedient and to forgive? Explain your response.

Have you ever experienced the Lord leading you to do something, and you obeyed? What was that experience like? How did you feel before and afterward?

Our willingness to forgive invites God to give us supernatural strength and provision. Through forgiveness we will be refreshed and renewed with hearts that are blessed through obedience.

Talk to God

Forgiving God, your kindness leads us to repentance. Thank you for your strong but gentle hand that guides and protects us. Help me to embrace forgiveness in my life and in my relationships. Help me to recognize the seeds of unforgiveness in my life and to surrender those to you. Thank you for your extravagant, all-encompassing love. Amen.

As You Go

How has this week's study on forgiveness spoken to your heart? How is God leading you to respond? What steps will you take? Journal your thoughts (pages provided at the end of the book).

VIDEO NOTES
A FEW MINUTES WITH MELODY

INTERESTING INSIGHTS:

POINTS I'D LIKE TO DISCUSS WITH THE GROUP:

WEEK 3
GOD'S WONDERFUL GRACE

Scripture for the Week

God won't always play the judge;
he won't be angry forever.
He doesn't deal with us according to our sin or repay us
according to our wrongdoing,
because as high as heaven is above the earth,
that's how large God's faithful love
is for those who honor him.
As far as east is from west—
that's how far God has removed
our sin from us.
Like a parent feels compassion for their children—
that's how the LORD feels compassion
for those who honor him.
Psalm 103:9–13

Excerpt from *River's Song,* Chapter 2

*T*he first raindrops began to fall, plunking noisily on the metal roof, as Anna searched in her handbag for the keys that the lawyer had given her that morning. He said the brass key was for the upstairs entrance and the stainless steel one was for the store below, but the brass key looked foreign to her. She couldn't remember anyone locking the door to their house while she was growing up. Sometimes Daddy didn't even bother to lock up the store. Despite a fairly steady cash flow in the store, except during the Great Depression, her parents had never seemed overly concerned about thieves or break-ins. Each night, her dad would stash the day's earnings in an old tin box that he kept tucked beneath his bed. But he had always been more careful when they made their weekly trip into town. Then he would place the cash in a money belt, "in case the boat sinks," he'd explain with a broad grin as he patted the slight bulge under his shirt. Of course, the boat never did sink. And the store never made their family wealthy either.

In fact, the store's income barely kept them clothed and fed during the Depression, but that wasn't so unusual; everyone had a tough time in those days. Each night at *supper, after Daddy said the blessing, he reminded them how fortunate they were to have food on the table and a roof over their head. Anna had been aware of Mother's black ledger book, where she recorded customers' cashless purchases, and that a fair amount of credit had been extended to their neighbors during those hard times. She also knew that customers sometimes paid their bills with an exchange of goods—and that could get interesting.*

As Anna worked the key into the stubborn lock she remembered the time Daddy had accepted a beautiful spinning wheel from Mrs. Sawyer. It was to cancel the Sawyer's rather large accumulation of debt. With tears in her eyes, Mrs. Sawyer had explained how her grandmother had brought the delicate item over by wagon train across the Oregon Trail. It was one of the few pieces to make it all the way to Oregon. Daddy kept the spinning wheel in a corner of the store right next to the potato bin, and every time Mrs. Sawyer came in she would head straight for it, running her hands over its polished surfaces. Daddy kept the spinning wheel for several years. He would occasionally get a generous offer from a collector wanting to purchase it. But each time he said, "Sorry, not for sale." Then one day, Mrs. Sawyer came in swinging her tattered purse and wearing a big smile. She made him a cash offer on the spinning wheel, explaining how she'd been saving up since they day she'd exchanged it. Daddy grinned and, refusing to take a profit, he sold it back to her for the exact same price that he'd wiped clean from her bill those many years before.

· · · · · · ·

DAY 1: THE GRACE OF GOD

Read God's Word

Jesus said, "A certain man had two sons. The younger son said to his father, 'Father, give me my share of the inheritance.' Then the father divided his estate between them. Soon afterward, the younger son gathered everything together and took a trip to a land far away. There, he wasted his wealth through extravagant living.

When he had used up his resources, a severe food shortage arose in that country and he began to be in need. He hired himself out to one of the citizens of that country, who sent him into his fields to feed pigs. He longed to eat his fill from what the pigs ate, but no one gave him anything. When he came to his senses, he said, 'How many of my father's hired hands have more than enough food, but I'm starving to death! I will get up and go to my father, and say to him, "Father, I have sinned against heaven and against you. I no longer deserve to be called your son. Take me on as one of your hired hands." '
So he got up and went to his father.

While he was still a long way off, his father saw him and was moved with compassion. His father ran to him, hugged him, and kissed him. Then his son said, 'Father, I have sinned against heaven and against you. I no longer deserve to be called your son.' But the father said to his servants, 'Quickly, bring out the best robe and put it on him! Put a ring on his finger and sandals on his feet! Fetch the fattened calf and slaughter it. We must celebrate with feasting because this son of mine was dead and has come back to life! He was lost and is found!' And they began to celebrate."

Luke 15:11-24

Reflect and Respond

In this story, often called The Parable of the Prodigal Son, Jesus tells of a greedy son and a gracious father. The son, consumed with a restlessness to get out of town and have some fun, eagerly takes his inheritance and promptly blows every last penny. Soon he is left with nothing, not even food to eat, and he longs to go home. But what will his father say? The son was disrespectful and greedy; he essentially disowned himself. He knows he deserves nothing, but he decides to take a chance and beg for mercy anyway.

He expects judgment, but what he gets is grace—and an eager grace at that, freely and joyfully given.

Our Father does the same for us: "See what great love the Father has lavished on us, that we should be called children of God!" (1 John 3:1 NIV) "Like a parent feels compassion for their children—that's how the LORD feels compassion for those who honor him" (Psalm 103:13).

> [The prodigal son] expects judgment, but what he gets is grace—and an eager grace at that, freely and joyfully given. Our Father does the same for us.

How do you relate to this parable?

How does it make you feel to know that God calls us His children?

What does being a parent require? Are these same things required of God, since God calls us His children?

61

How does our rebellion affect our relationship with God? How does it affect us?

Often we must reach the end of ourselves—of our own resources and abilities and efforts—in order to receive God's grace. It is in those moments we learn that in our helplessness, God is strong.

Anna has great hopes for having a strong relationship with her daughter, Lauren; but once Anna moves back to the river and begins to challenge Eunice's influence on their lives, Lauren begins to pull away even more. Anna hopes that if Lauren comes to visit her on the river, they will have the opportunity to reconnect and share in the vision of the inn; but just when that seems possible, Anna feels her daughter slipping through her fingers once again.

Excerpt from *River's Song,* Chapter 24

Anna tried to conceal her heartbreak during dinner. She planned to let her friends know [about the fight with her daughter and] about her disappointment that Lauren wouldn't be coming—later—because she knew that if she opened the dam right now all her emotions would come raging out and ruin the meal for everyone. And so she was quiet.

[But as everyone chatted,] Anna set her fork down on the plate of barely touched food. "I'm sorry," she said quietly. "Will you, please, excuse me?" Then she stood and hurried to her room, closing the door behind her. She sat down on the bed, wringing her hands as tears silently slipped down her cheeks. She wished she'd gone outside instead of getting stuck in her room, which suddenly felt claustrophobic. She considered going out again, bolting for the door, but she did not want her friends to see her like this. She felt powerless and miserable, and totally incapable of running this inn. Really, what had made her think she had the strength to do such a thing? She thought she was strong, but in reality, she was weak. Very weak.

Anna remembered something her grandmother used to say. "When I am weak, I am strong." The first time Anna heard it she'd been confused, asking what it meant. Grandma Pearl said the words were from God's book. "It means when I run out, when I am empty and weak, God can fill me. I must be empty first."

As she cried alone in her little room, Anna felt as if she were being emptied. And yet the tears continued to flow—as if there were a deep well inside of her, full of sadness and loss and disappointment—and it was all pouring out tonight. After a while she fell asleep, then waking she realized it was dark out. The house was quiet. Her guests must've gone to bed. She thought about her grandmother's words again. Anna had no doubts she was being emptied, but she wondered what it took to get filled back up, like Grandma had said, with God. "Ask and the Creator gives," Grandma used to say. Sometimes she'd say this in reference to good weather or catching a big fish or finding a bountiful spot to gather blackberries or pickle weed. But tonight Anna decided to take this to heart. She would ask the Creator to give her what she needed—and she would ask him now. And so she prayed for strength. "Give me your strength," she prayed. "I feel I've run out of my own. I am empty. Please, fill me up." It was a very simple prayer—but from the heart—and when she finished, she felt her sense of peace returning to her. And she felt energized.

· · · · · · ·

Has there ever been a time when you felt completely empty and helpless? Where did you turn?

What did you learn from being in that helpless, empty place?

Talk to God

Abba Father, I am so grateful that I can call you my Father. Thank you for loving, protecting, disciplining, and comforting me. Help me to have a willing heart, and take away any rebellion in my soul. I praise you for your abundant grace. Amen.

As You Go

Reflect and meditate on 1 John 3:1 today:

See what great love the Father has lavished on us, that we should be called children of God! And that is what we are! (NIV)

> "Anna had no doubts she was being emptied, but she wondered what it took to get filled back up, like Grandma had said, with God. 'Ask and the Creator gives,' Grandma used to say. . . . Tonight Anna decided to take this to heart."

DAY 2: REFLECTING HIS GLORY

Read God's Word

"You have heard that it was said, 'You shall love your neighbor and hate your enemy.' But I say to you, love your enemies and pray for those who persecute you."

Matthew 5:43-44 NASB

Reflect and Respond

As beloved children of God, we are lavished with love and grace. In turn, we are free to be generous and gracious with others.

What might it look like, practically speaking, to extend grace to others? What are some situations you can think of?

Can you think of a time when someone extended grace to you? How did it affect your life?

Sometimes extending grace to another requires sacrifice on our part, as illustrated by one of Grandma Pearl's stories.

Excerpt from *River's Song,* Chapter 12

Hazel was flushed with excitement when she came to dinner. "Oh, I just translated the most wonderful story of your grandmother's." And as they ate, Hazel went on to tell the story of why the river sparkles like stars. Of course, the tale was very familiar, but Anna didn't say anything because she could see how much Hazel was enjoying herself.

"Long, long ago," Hazel launched into the telling, "The tribe on one side of the river owned all the stars in the sky, and naturally the tribe on the other side wanted the stars for themselves."

"Naturally." Anna smiled as she passed Hazel the peas.

"Fortunately, neither tribe was particularly warlike, but they were not opposed to sneaking over in the middle of the night to quietly steal the stars from each other." Hazel

As beloved children of God, we are lavished with love and grace. In turn, we are free to be generous and gracious with others.

chuckled. "And these moonlight raids went on for some time, the two tribes stealing the stars back and forth until I suppose even the stars were confused. Then one time, the tribe who were the original owners of the stars had the stars back in their custody again, and they didn't want to lose them. So that night they all stayed awake—waiting for the star thieves to arrive."

Now Hazel lowered her voice, very much like Grandma Pearl used to do. "And they watched from behind the trees as the thieves once again stole their stars. Only this time the original owners followed the thieves, finally stopping them at the river. Well the original owners must've been quite fed up because on this night, a great battle arose with both tribes fighting over who rightfully owned the stars." Hazel paused to catch her breath.

"And the stars were caught in the middle of the battle," Anna continued for her in a dramatic voice, "And they didn't like to see the fighting, so hundreds of the stars leaped from the sky, plummeting right into the river. And the rest of the stars spread themselves out so there would be enough for everyone and so the people would quit fighting. And to this day, that is why the river sparkles like there are stars in it."

Hazel grinned. "That is right!"

"I used to love that story." Anna split open a biscuit. "It was my favorite bedtime story. I loved that the stars would do that just to bring peace."

"It's a lovely story. And one I've never heard before." Hazel reached for the butter. "And it reminded me of Clark and Gloria and Marshall."

"Is Gloria Clark's wife?"

"Ex-wife." Hazel frowned. "But when she left Clark for Larry back when Marshall was only six, there was a custody battle for Marshall. Naturally, the mother won—mothers almost always do. But the problem was that she and Larry wanted to move down here to Oregon for his work, which seemed unfair since Clark was building homes up near Seattle."

"That does seem unfair."

"So Clark was like the stars in your grandmother's story—he made the sacrifice, sold his business, and moved down here and started all over again, just so he could still be near his boy."

· · · · · · ·

Sometimes choosing to extend grace requires a sacrifice and a willingness to allow the other person to "win."

Sometimes choosing to extend grace requires a sacrifice and a willingness to allow the other person to "win." What does Clark's willingness to extend grace to his ex-wife and son require of him?

How might his choice affect his relationship with his son?

When we choose to extend grace to others, how does that reflect the grace of God?

> It is considerably easier to extend grace to someone we love and respect than it is to extend grace to someone who has hurt us. . . . Yet Jesus doesn't let our hearts off the hook when dealing with those people.

I can recall several situations where I was wronged by someone in a position of "authority" over me. And often it was by someone who was supposed to be a Christian. The first time this happened to me I was shocked and outraged—how dare a Christian act like that? And in my naivety and youth, I decided to confront this person in a "scriptural" way. But when I got less than nowhere, I was confused, and the temptation was to remain angry and hurt. I eventually learned that despite this person's bad behavior, it was still my responsibility to forgive. And I realized that I needed God's help to do this. The best part of this lesson was what followed after I made the choice to forgive (although the person was probably oblivious to the grace I was offering): a heavy burden was lifted from my shoulders and I was freed from bondage to this person, and well on my way toward healing. Over time it became easier to forgive others.

It is considerably easier to extend grace to someone we love and respect than it is to extend grace to someone who has hurt us. In Matthew 5:43–44, Jesus says, "You have heard that it was said, 'You shall love your neighbor and hate your enemy.' But I say to you, love your enemies and pray for those who persecute you" (NASB).

Enemy, defined as "one seeking to injure, overthrow, or confound an opponent," is not a label we often use in conversation, but that doesn't mean we don't deal with people in our lives who seem intent on hurting and discouraging us. Yet Jesus doesn't let our hearts off the hook when dealing with those people: "For if you love those who love you, what reward do you have? Do not even the tax collectors do the same?" (v. 46 NASB)

Have you ever offered grace to someone who didn't "deserve" it? What happened?

How can the gift of God's grace help us to forgive even those who wish us harm?

Talk to God

Lord, the grace you extend to us is unfathomable and unattainable. Though I could never match your gift of grace, help me to have a gracious heart, one that is committed to reflecting your glory. Open my eyes and help me to see those to whom I need to extend grace and forgiveness. Amen.

As You Go

What is one tangible way you can extend grace to someone today? If nothing comes to mind, watch for an opportunity throughout the day.

DAY 3: GRACE IN GOD'S TIMING

Read God's Word

He who began a good work in you will carry it on to completion until the day of Christ Jesus.

Philippians 1:6 NIV

And we know that in all things God works for the good of those who love him, who have been called according to his purpose.

Romans 8:28 NIV

Reflect and Respond

Timing is everything, they say. So often it seems that the thing we've been waiting for…and waiting for…and waiting for just never seems to happen. Whether you're waiting for the dream job to materialize, or that person to ask you out on a date, or to finally just get clarity on a situation, waiting can be an uncomfortable, disheartening process. Though we pray diligently and earnestly, sometimes it seems that God is silent, and all we can do is wait.

Waiting is not something that comes easily for most of us. In fact, we go to great lengths to make sure we don't have to wait for much of anything these days. Our culture thrives on instant gratification. Sending a Tweet or e-mail can get us a response in mere minutes—sometimes even seconds. A swipe of the debit card and we are out the door in record time with our purchase. And if we don't want to go to the store, online shopping guarantees we never have to wait in line.

So what happens when we can't get what we want, when we want it? That's not something we can easily handle, is it? We get anxious, irritable, depressed, angry, and sometimes even hopeless.

How do you handle having to wait for something?

When we trust that God will do what He says—that He will complete His work in us and work everything for our good—we are able to wait well, to choose to trust that God's wisdom and timing are perfect.

What is something you are waiting for in your life right now? How are you reacting to the waiting?

Theologians often describe God as *omniscient,* meaning God resides outside of time and has knowledge and understanding that is infinite. In other words, God doesn't work on our time but rather operates from a vantage point that sees the whole picture.

In today's Scripture verses from Philippians and Romans, we read that God will complete the good work He began in each of us and will work all things for our good because we love Him and are called according to His purpose.

Review Philippians 1:6 and Romans 8:28. How do these verses make you feel? How do they speak to your waiting?

When we trust that God will do what He says—that He will complete His work in us and work everything for our good—we are able to *wait well,* to choose to trust that God's wisdom and timing are perfect.

What might it mean to "wait well"? How might waiting well affect our actions, words, and thoughts?

What might it look like for you to wait well for God's perfect timing?

For many years, Anna had no hope that her life could be any different. Her dreams were stifled and her confidence shaken in the years after Adam returned home from the war, and she didn't have the courage to believe in a second chance at a new life. Though her heart longed for companionship, she was isolated and alone. But once she returns to the river and begins once again to believe in the power of love and healing, her heart is open and ready to receive the gift of romance—of Clark—into her life.

Excerpt from *River's Song,* Chapter 25

Anna was surprised to hear the sound of a motor interrupting the stillness of a sunny afternoon—but it wasn't coming from the river. She dropped the hoe she'd been using and walked over to the other side of the house—and there was Clark's blue pickup driving through the meadow. An unexpected surge of joy rushed through her, and she felt her cheeks flush. He was back!

"Welcome back," she called as he hopped out of the pickup.

He looked intently at her, his deep blue eyes shining brightly. "It's so good to see you, Anna. It feels like it's been a lot longer than a week and a half."

"I know." She glanced down at her dirt encrusted fingernails then shoved her hands into her pockets.

"I hadn't planned it like this, Anna, but...oh well, why not?"

"What?" She felt puzzled.

Clark took in a deep breath then reached into his shirt pocket and cleared his throat. "I wanted to plan something more special, Anna, something old fashioned and memorable." To her stunned surprise, he now removed a small blue velvet box and got down on one knee, looking up at her with the most sincere expression she had ever seen. "The truth is I knew from the start that I would do this, Anna, I just had no idea how soon I would actually do it."

Anna felt slightly faint and a bit dizzy as she stared down at him. What on earth was he thinking? Why was he doing this?

"Anna, I love you." He looked directly into her eyes. "I know, you're probably shocked by this—I wouldn't blame you if you turned me down, but I love you, Anna. I love you so much that every day spent away from you was pure misery. I had no idea I could love someone this much, but I do. You don't have to answer me right now, because I can tell by your face you're in complete shock. But, I still have to ask you. Dear Anna, will you marry me?"

Her hand flew up to her mouth, but no words came out.

He looked worried now. "I know, I know. I'm doing this all wrong." He slowly stood, still holding the small box in his big hands. "I didn't mean to do it like this. I'm not usually the impulsive type. Not that this is an impulse, Anna. It certainly is not."

So many things were racing through her mind now. She had sworn she'd never jump hastily into marriage again. And she had promised herself she would never leave this river. But as she looked into his eyes, all she could think was that she loved him too.

"Oh, Clark," she finally said. It was all that would come out.

"I know my eagerness has probably overwhelmed you." He started to open the little blue box now. "But since I've gone ahead and plunged right in, I might as well finish it. I really did have a plan . . . of sorts."

He opened the box and held it out for her to see. Anna's eyes grew large as she stared down at the biggest pearl she'd ever seen with a smaller diamond next to it. Set in what appeared to be platinum, the ring was beautiful. "Oh, my!" was all she could mutter.

"I was inspired by your grandparents' story, thinking about how John couldn't find the right pearl for her, it reminded me of another story. The story of a man who found an amazing pearl—the most magnificent pearl in the world—and he went home and sold everything he owned just so he could go back and purchase the incredible pearl. Well, Anna, that's how I feel about you. When I found you, I knew you were amazing, incredible, wonderful. I knew I would give up everything, I would sell everything, I would do anything—just to have you say yes to me."

"Oh, Clark," she spoke quietly, looking from the pearl to his eyes, knowing that she was going to throw her earlier resolve to the wind. "I love you too. My answer is yes, Clark, most assuredly yes."

He wrapped his arms around her and, pulling her close, he kissed her solidly— and she kissed him back, intensely and with all the longing that had been building in her. It was a long wonderful kiss—and like a perfect pearl, she knew she would treasure it forever.

"Oh, my!" she exclaimed when he finally released her. She honestly thought she was seeing stars and her head felt light. "It's perfect."

• • • • • • •

Not only did Anna receive the gift of love, she received a gift of extravagant love. The gift was unexpected, but perfect nonetheless.

What might God be doing in the waiting you are experiencing now? How might God be shaping a perfect gift for you?

Read 1 Corinthians 2:9. How does this verse encourage you today?

Talk to God

Dear God, you know me well. You know my heart and my desires and my needs, and you know when those will be fulfilled or changed for the better. Give me eyes to see your dreams for me. Give me ears to hear your voice in my waiting. Amen.

As You Go

Choose one of the verses discussed today and post it somewhere you will see it often, as a reminder of God's love and purposes for you.

DAY 4: GRACE IN OUR SPEECH

Walk into any café at lunchtime and you will no doubt see a table of women sitting, eating lunch, and talking. There's no getting around it—we women like to talk. We talk about our kids, our husbands, our homes, our work, our favorite magazines and TV shows. You name the topic, and, if we're so inclined, we have much to say about it.

God made women to be relational, with an inherent need to be known and understood and a desire to know others as well. And that requires talking! Consider what God's word has to say about our words.

Read God's Word

Do not let any unwholesome talk come out of your mouths, but only what is helpful for building others up according to their needs, that it may benefit those who listen.

Ephesians 4:29 NIV

Her mouth is full of wisdom; kindly teaching is on her tongue.

Proverbs 31:26

A gentle answer turns away wrath, but a harsh word stirs up anger. The tongue of the wise adorns knowledge, but the mouth of the fool gushes folly.

Proverbs 15:1-2

Those who consider themselves religious and yet do not keep a tight rein on their tongues deceive themselves, and their religion is worthless.

James 1:26 NIV

Even though the tongue is a small part of the body, it boasts wildly. Think about this: a small flame can set a whole forest on fire. The tongue is a small flame of fire, a world of evil at work in us. It contaminates our entire lives.

James 3:5–6

Reflect and Respond

These Scriptures remind us that our words carry weight and meaning for the people in our lives, and it is important for us to understand the impact our words can have.

Based on these verses, how do you think God feels about our speech?

How do these verses instruct us on using our speech well?

Circle the Scripture that speaks most strongly to you today. What is God saying to you through these words?

In *River's Song,* we see just how powerfully words can affect our relationships, and we see this most clearly in Anna, who is shaped by both Eunice's and Hazel's words. While Eunice's sharp tongue and hateful words have plagued and degraded Anna for many years, Hazel's words of grace and encouragement build Anna up and allow her the grace to believe in second chances. Eunice spitefully called Anna "Squaw Woman" and insulted her appearance and her family roots, but Hazel celebrated Anna's Indian heritage and its culture of resourcefulness and strong women.

Take some time to consider the words you use. How do you speak to your spouse? your children? your coworkers? your friends?

Are you quick to speak grace and truth, or do you struggle with being critical and harsh? What emotions and beliefs may be fueling your words?

How might your speech be affecting those who are close to you?

Because God is gracious and kind with us, we are free to extend kind words to others. Proverbs 15:1 says, "A gentle answer turns away wrath" (NASB). Daily we come upon pivotal moments that allow us a choice about how to respond to others. An apathetic store clerk is rude. A distracted driver cuts us off in traffic. The person on the other end of the line just isn't helping us get what we want. Your sister brings up the old family argument again.

Most often our first response is to lash out in anger and frustration when our feelings are hurt or our pride is wounded. We want things to be easy and comfortable; we want people to be kind and respectful. But if we can respond in graciousness and kindness, our words can have healing, transformative power in the lives of others.

Were you ever in a situation where your words spoke judgment? Explain.

Were you ever in a situation where your words spoke love? Explain.

Where is God leading you to extend grace to someone else today through your words?

Anna's journey of transformation is filled with small graces extended to her by others. Based on what you have read thus far of Anna's journey, can you name some of those kindnesses?

Most often our first response is to lash out in anger and frustration when our feelings are hurt or our pride is wounded. . . . But if we can respond in graciousness and kindness, our words can have healing, transformative power in the lives of others.

It is not always easy for Anna to accept and receive the kind words and gestures of others. Why do you think this is so?

Do you relate to Anna in that way? Are you able to receive words of grace from others? Why or why not?

"There is a time for everything . . . a time for keeping silent, and a time for speaking." (Ecclesiastes 3:1, 7)

Talk to God

Jesus, please reign over my speech. Help me to withhold harsh words born in anger and frustration and to freely speak words that flow from your grace. Help me to ask forgiveness from others when my words wound, and give me the grace to change my bad habits. Thank you for the beautiful words you speak over me every day. Thank you that your mercies are new every day. Amen.

As You Go

Pray and meditate on Ecclesiastes 3:1,7: "There is a time for everything . . . a time for keeping silent, and a time for speaking." How is God speaking to you today?

DAY 5: GRACE IN THE EVERYDAY

Read God's Word

"Because of the LORD's great love we are not consumed, for his compassions never fail. They are new every morning; great is your faithfulness."

Lamentations 3:22-23 NIV

Reflect and Respond

Moments of grace, both extended and received, surround us every day. They are found in the quiet, early morning cup of coffee, the kiss on a child's tear-stained cheek, the acknowledgment of a hurt feeling or a stressful situation, a well-timed hug and listening ear, the early morning light that once again makes the world new.

These small kindnesses and mercies are abundant, but often we don't have eyes to see them. Our days are so filled with noise and busyness and to-dos that it is hard for us to stop and see that the Lord is good and is always taking care of us.

Today's verses from Lamentations remind us that God is ever faithful; God's love and grace surround us at all times.

Take a few moments to think about your day thus far. For what can you be grateful? How has God extended His vast mercy and grace to you today?

Can you recall a time when you rejected or did not acknowledge that grace? If so, describe it.

> Our days are so filled with noise and busyness and to-dos that it is hard for us to stop and see that the Lord is good and is always taking care of us.

Jesus said, *"Who among you will give your children a stone when they ask for bread? Or give them a snake when they ask for fish? If you who are evil know how to give good gifts to your children, how much more will your heavenly Father give good things to those who ask him"* (Matthew 7:9-11).

This verse reassures us that God will take care of us, that He is watching and waiting to bless us with every good thing.

Do you ever stop and ask God to bless you throughout the day?

When are you most aware of the presence of God during your day? How do you acknowledge those times?

Even when we are unaware of God's provision and love, He is working in our lives, perfecting His perfect will for us. Like Anna's grandfather, John, God doesn't settle for anything less for the one He loves.

Excerpt from *River's Song,* Chapter 24

Even when we are unaware of God's provision and love, He is working in our lives, perfecting His perfect will for us.

Hazel stood. "Before I turn in for the night, I'd like to tell a final story—one that I transcribed recently. I found this one particularly touching because it seems that it's a true story about something that really happened to Anna's grandmother."

"Really?" Anna was intrigued.

"That's my best guess. Perhaps you've heard it before." Now she began to tell about a time when [Grandma] Pearl was a girl. "I'm guessing she was about sixteen," Hazel clarified. "They were on their way home from the reservation and Pearl must've been a pretty girl—perhaps like Anna here, only younger. Somewhere along the way, perhaps even on the reservation, Pearl had caught the eye of a young man named John."

"My grandfather," Anna said.

"Yes. And the reason I know your grandmother was attractive, well, besides the old photo you showed me, is because there were quite a few young women traveling in the group—and it seems the men were rather limited in number so John could afford to be choosy. Apparently John was very interested in your grandmother. Trying hard to get her attention and not succeeding. But she was being coy or playing hard to get, or perhaps she was simply shy. So one morning John went out to forage for food and he returned to camp with a big bag of oysters. And as he shucked the oysters, he found a number of pearls.

"Yes!" Anna exclaimed, "I do remember this story."

"Perhaps you'd like to finish it." Hazel looked hopeful. "I'd love to hear your version."

Anna nodded then, following Hazel's example, she too stood. "I hope I can get this right. Like Hazel said, my grandfather, John, was finding some pearls as he shucked the oysters. So he gave these pearls to the other girls traveling with them. But he didn't give a single one to my grandmother—whose name happened to be Pearl."

Hazel chuckled. "And Pearl was none too happy about it either."

"In fact she was downright angry about being slighted like that." Anna folded her arms across her front as if she too were mad. "Pearl glared at John then stomped off down the beach until she found a rock where she sat down and pouted alone."

"Then what happened?" Marshall asked eagerly.

"John went and found Pearl and then asked her why she was so angry."

"He did not know?" Babette looked skeptical.

"Maybe he did. Anyway, Pearl demanded to know why John had given the pearls to all the other girls, but had given none to her. Especially after he'd acted so interested in her. She told him he was a mean, mean man."

"What did he say about that?" Marshall asked.

"John told her that the pearls were worthless."

"Worthless?" Babette looked shocked.

"It seems the pearls were misshapen and flawed and not fully formed," Anna explained. "John told my grandmother that he'd hoped to find at least one smooth lovely pearl to present to her. But he'd been disappointed to find none of them were good enough for her. He explained that it would be wrong to present a less than perfect pearl to a perfect Pearl."

· · · · · · ·

Like a perfect pearl, God's grace is complete and not lacking in anything. It is all that we need, the perfect fulfillment of His love for us.

In imparting what is known as The Lord's Prayer to His disciples, Jesus said,

"Your Father knows what you need before you ask. Pray like this: Our Father who is in heaven, uphold the holiness of your name. Bring in your kingdom so that your will is done on earth as it's done in heaven. Give us the bread we need for today. Forgive us for the ways we have wronged you, just as we also forgive those who have wronged us. And don't lead us into temptation, but rescue us from the evil one."

Matthew 6:8–13

What do you think it means to ask God for "the bread we need for today"?

Read Exodus 16. How did God provide for the Israelites' needs as they wandered in the desert?

Are you aware that you need to ask for God's strength daily, and do you do this? Why or why not?

In what areas do you find you need the most grace and strength?

> Like a perfect pearl, God's grace is complete and not lacking in anything. It is all that we need, the perfect fulfillment of His love for us.

Talk to God

Heavenly Father, thank you that your mercies are new every day. You recognize that we are weak and forgetful, and that we need to be reminded—often—that you are attentive to our needs. You know what I need, Lord, and you will be faithful to provide. Thank you for your faithful love. Amen.

As You Go

Recite out loud The Lord's Prayer:

"Our Father in heaven, hallowed be your name, your kingdom come, your will be done, on earth as it is in heaven. Give us today our daily bread. And forgive us our debts, as we also have forgiven our debtors. And lead us not into temptation, but deliver us from the evil one."

Matthew 6:9-13 NIV

How has God provided for you today? Reflect on this throughout the day. As you have time, journal your thoughts (journaling pages are provided at the back of the book).

VIDEO NOTES
A FEW MINUTES WITH MELODY

INTERESTING INSIGHTS:

POINTS I'D LIKE TO DISCUSS WITH THE GROUP:

THEME 2

Healing Relationships

River's Call

BEFORE YOU BEGIN

Book Summary: *River's Call*

River's Call opens with Anna and Clark returning from their honeymoon. It is 1959, and Anna's first fall on the river in twenty years, and she is excited about getting her cabins set up and opening the Inn at Shining Waters. When an ill Lauren calls, Anna insists that she come to the river to recuperate. Soon they discover that Lauren is pregnant with her boyfriend Donald's baby. Lauren is distraught, as is Donald, who had already moved on to someone new, and Eunice is livid. Soon Eunice comes to the inn, along with Donald and his mother, and she hatches a plan to have the two elope immediately and settle back in Pine Ridge. Anna isn't sure that is the best plan, but Lauren and Donald get married and move into Eunice's house.

The next summer a baby girl, Sarah Pearl, is born, and Anna immediately falls in love with Sarah. Anna stays in Pine Ridge for a few days to help Lauren and baby adjust, and while there she discovers that Donald and Lauren's relationship is precarious at best. Anna encourages them to get out of Eunice's house and find a place of their own. While Donald settles into their new home, Lauren and Sarah come and stay with Anna at the river for a while where Lauren gets help and encouragement from Anna, Babette, and Hazel. When Anna returns to Pine Ridge a few months later to visit, she finds Lauren moving out of her house and back into Eunice's, where Eunice has hired a nanny to lure Lauren and Donald back into her home with promises of help and comfort.

Over the next few years, Anna tries to entice Lauren to bring the baby out to the river to visit, but Lauren always makes excuses, and Anna only sees Sarah occasionally. As Sarah's fifth birthday approaches, they finally come to the river to visit the inn, which has continued to evolve and improve. Anna quickly realizes that things are not going well in Lauren's household. She discovers that Lauren is lazy and practically ignores Sarah, preferring to shop and redecorate their house. After becoming fed up with Lauren's apathy and neglect, a confrontation ensues and Anna kicks Lauren out of the inn. Almost a year later, Sarah comes to stay at the river for the summer while Lauren and Eunice go to Europe. Anna and Sarah have an instant connection and enjoy a wonderful summer together. But Anna continues to be concerned about Lauren, who seems very depressed and is drinking and taking pills.

As fall fades into winter, Anna realizes that Babette is aging, and so she invites her to come and stay at the inn for the winter. Babette dies in the spring, leaving everything—including her charming house—to Anna, who decides to keep and repair it.

After Anna spends another wonderful summer on the river with Sarah, Eunice calls and says she and Sarah want to come for a weekend in November. During that surprise visit, a corner is turned in Anna and Eunice's relationship when Eunice admits that she has been very bitter toward Anna because of Adam. Eunice explains that Adam's father, who was a cruel man, died when Adam was young, and after that Eunice felt Adam was all she had left in the world. When Adam married Anna, Eunice felt Anna had stolen him from her, and when he returned home from the war, broken and depressed, Eunice felt that she lost him all over again; so she took out her hurt on Anna. Eunice apologizes and Anna realizes that they were both in pain for many years over losing Adam. Having finally released years of bitterness, Eunice passes away just after Christmas.

Over the next few years, Sarah continues to come to the river each summer. Anna loves it, and enjoys a close relationship with Sarah. In the summer of 1975, Sarah tells Anna that her dad is having an affair, and she's afraid her mom is taking too many pills. Though seemingly wise and stable beyond her fifteen years, Anna worries about Sarah's lack of a stable, happy family.

In the winter, Lauren calls, despondent and depressed. Having been through rehab for pills and alcohol, she has hit rock bottom but feels that the river is calling to her. She comes to the river the next day and reveals that Donald has left her for another woman. Later, when Anna's canoe disappears, a frantic search ensues for Lauren. After several tense hours, they find a waterlogged and scared Lauren in Babette's house. After nearly drowning when the canoe capsized, Lauren is shaken, but she is now determined to live and to change her life for the better.

Lauren stays on at the river through the spring; she turns a corner in her life and hopes that things can be different. But when Sarah doesn't want to come to the river for the summer, Anna and Lauren are surprised and worried. Before long, Donald calls to say that sixteen-year-old Sarah has run off with her boyfriend after a fight about his affair, and he doesn't know where she is. Though both women are distraught at the thought of losing Sarah, they believe that her strength will protect her and pray that her strength will bring her home.

Character Sketches

Lauren

Lauren (Anna's daughter) was born pre–World War II. Her father, Adam, returned home from the war with severe injuries, including depression and mood swings—known as Post Traumatic Stress Disorder today; however, at that time, PTSD was less-understood and rarely treated. Because of Adam's challenges and financial troubles, Eunice pressured the young family to move into her big house. There, Eunice took over raising Lauren (by spoiling her rotten), and Anna was forced into a subservient role as cook, nurse, and housekeeper. As a result, Lauren is self-centered, shallow, immature, and selfish, and her relationship with her mother (Anna) is severely impaired. She sees her grandma (Eunice) disrespecting Anna, and she learns to do the same. Lauren's been taught that life should be fun and that she should always be the center of attention and have whatever she wants. She goes to college with this mindset, gets pregnant, marries, and then reality quickly sets in. Thanks to Anna's gracious spirit, Lauren gets her second chance (and third and fourth) when she visits her mother on the river. It takes time and hard knocks (and Anna's mercy) for Lauren to grow up, but she eventually does. Unfortunately, while she is struggling to grow up, she severely neglects her own daughter, Sarah.

Eunice

Eunice (Anna's mother-in-law) grew up poor and pretty. Because of her good looks and her pushy mother, she was married off into the richest family in town. But, her husband didn't love her and he wasn't faithful; he was also a cruel, hard taskmaster. Eunice suffered silently until he died. Then, she took over the family business and turned into a controlling, hard woman. She resented her only son's marriage to Anna and she resented Anna's Indian heritage, making no attempt to hide her bigotry. As much as Eunice hurt others, she hurt herself. Her life was superficial and miserable. It's not until she's at the end of her life, while visiting Anna on the river, that she confronts and confesses these things. Her lifetime of bitter unforgiveness has been like poison to her. Before Eunice's death, Anna helps her to see the power of forgiving others.

Donald

Donald is the small town "golden boy" who's been a bit spoiled and entitled. Athletic and attractive, he had a string of girlfriends during high school and a reputation for being a user. He's shallow and self-centered with no interest in getting married when Lauren gets pregnant. However, he slowly grows up (faster than his wife) and is a good provider, although through a job he dislikes. He loves his daughter, Sarah, in his own way, but is not an exemplary father by any means. Eventually, when Lauren gets trapped in her addictions, Donald strays from his marriage and enters into an affair that leads to further neglect of his daughter and eventual divorce.

WEEK 4
RESTORING RELATIONSHIPS

Scripture for the Week

*The L*ORD *works righteousness;*
does justice for all who are oppressed.
God made his ways known to Moses;
made his deeds known to the Israelites.
*The L*ORD *is compassionate*
and merciful, very patient, and full of faithful love.
Psalm 103:6–8

Excerpt from *River's Call*, Chapter 18

*A*nna *didn't know what to say.*

"Really, I want to throw in the towel. I want out of this. I want to be a carefree college coed again. I was robbed of all that and I want it back!" Lauren groaned loudly.

"What about Sarah?" Anna asked. "Don't you love her?"

"Of course, I love her. She is the only reason I'm doing all this, Mom. If it weren't for Sarah and the fact that she needs a daddy, I would get on a bus going somewhere far, far from here. And sometimes I honestly think she might be better off if we both just left him for good."

"Really?"

There was a long pause now. "I don't know, Mom. . . . I mean, I guess I really do love Donald . . . despite all his faults and there are plenty of them. I'm probably making this seem worse than it is. But sometimes when I see him coming home in his suit and tie, well, I sort of forget how mad I am at him."

"Then I suppose you're going to just have to try harder, Lauren."

"Maybe so. . . ."

"I wish we lived closer, sweetie. I wish I could come give you a hand."

"Me too." She sniffed loudly.

"Things are slowing down at the inn. . . . Maybe I could come for a little visit."

"Really?"

"Let me talk to Clark about it."

"Oh, Mom, if you could do that—oh, it would make all the difference in the world.

I know it would! This place is tiny, but I could put a cot in Sarah's room. If you wouldn't mind."

"I wouldn't mind at all."

"Oh, please, don't just think about it. Please, do it!"

"I'll let you know. In the meantime, don't forget to take the roast out of the oven."

"Right. I better go get it now. I think I can smell smoke."

"I love you, Lauren. Give Sarah a kiss for me." As [Anna] hung up the phone, she hoped that the roast wasn't burning. Poor Lauren. Sometimes she was really her own worst enemy.

Anna and Clark discussed a visit, looked at the reservations book, and finally found a patch of three days during the first week of October when no guests were booked. "Why don't you go then?" he suggested. "That's just over a week away."

"You wouldn't mind?"

"Not a bit. Maybe I'll even go with you."

"I'll call Lauren in the morning and tell her the good news." She hugged him. "I can't wait to see Sarah!"

"And your daughter?"

She chuckled. "Of course, I want to see Lauren too. It's just that she's a bit more difficult than the baby."

He nodded. "I must agree with you on that."

Anna knew that no matter how difficult Lauren could be, no matter how selfish or immature, she would always be her daughter and Anna would never give up on her. But for Lauren's sake, she wished she'd grow up.

Lauren sounded very relieved to hear her mother was planning a trip to Pine Ridge. "But can't you come any sooner?" she pleaded.

"Do your best, sweetie. If you get frustrated, put Sarah in her stroller and go for a walk, enjoy the fall foliage. And before you know it, I'll be there."

Lauren made a few more gloomy comments and Anna told her it was time to start fixing lunch. After she hung up, Anna shook her head and wondered if someday Lauren would wake up, come to her senses, and realize all the goodness that was in her life.

For Anna the days passed quickly and soon she and Clark were on their way to Pine Ridge.

"Lauren is so frustrated . . . I just hope I can be of help," Anna said.

"If you can't help her, I don't know who can."

"She said that she feels like she has two children. Sarah and Donald."

He chuckled.

"I remember feeling like that too." She sighed, twisting the handkerchief that was in her lap. "When Adam came home from the war, he was a lot like a child."

"You mean because of his physical injuries?"

"Partly. He needed a lot of help doing things. His mind was like a child in some ways too. Not that his brain was damaged per se. But his spirit was . . . well, it seemed that it was destroyed."

"War did that to some men."

"And when I think back on it, the way he acted—somewhat selfishly and childishly—it reminds me a little of how Lauren acts sometimes. Not always . . . but sometimes."

"She is Adam's daughter."

"It's strange, isn't it? She never really knew her father. Not really. And yet she may be more like him than she is like me...even though she's known me all her life." She shook her head. "But, to be fair, she never really knew the real me. She saw a shadow of me, an intimidated me, the poor little woman me...the pitiful creature that Eunice walked all over." She felt a bit teary. "I was such a poor example to Lauren, Clark. Sometimes I feel completely to blame for all her problems."

"I've told you before, you can't blame yourself for the way you raised Lauren, Anna, not any more than you can blame yourself for what happened to Adam." He reached over and patted her hand. "I know you, and I can't believe you weren't doing the best you could . . . under some very hard circumstances."

She nodded. "I know that's true. But it's hard not to feel guilty." She turned and looked at him. "Do you think all mothers feel guilty?"

"Someday Lauren is going to figure out how strong you are, Anna, how you've always been strong. And I think she'll want to be like you."

· · · · · · · ·

DAY 1: BEAUTY IN RESTORATION

Read God's Word

So then, if anyone is in Christ, that person is part of the new creation. The old things have gone away, and look, new things have arrived! All of these new things are from God, who reconciled us to himself through Christ and who gave us the ministry of reconciliation. In other words, God was reconciling the world to himself through Christ, by not counting people's sins against them. He has trusted us with this message of reconciliation. So we are ambassadors who represent Christ. God is negotiating with you through us. We beg you as Christ's representatives, "Be reconciled to God!"

2 Corinthians 5:17-20

Reflect and Respond

Sometimes old things seem to cry out to be made new again. When Anna returns to her parents' home after so many years away, she sees the potential in its comfortable, yet humble, state. Once a thriving general store that was a vital part of the community, Anna longs to make the home a gathering place once more, to see the property become a refuge and a place of healing and rest.

There is something about a once-majestic old house that calls out for restoration—for its worn and dusty bannister to be dusted and polished, its tarnished floors to be refinished so they once again shine, its cloudy, cracked windows to be replaced so that sunlight pours in . . . for someone to see the beauty amidst the ruins and to restore what has been lost.

When you see a home that has been restored, you can't help but be impressed by the time, patience, resources, and energy that were involved in the transformation. It is amazing to know that someone had a vision for a sagging, weatherworn house and carried it out with a passion to restore and make it inviting again. You can't help but appreciate the beauty that has been won through hard work.

Often there are relationships in our lives that are like these old houses—decimated by storms, worn down by circumstance, dusty and crumbling from neglect. But there is hope for these relationships, for our God is one who desires restoration and reconciliation.

Are there any relationships in your life that need reviving? What do you think needs to happen for those relationships to be restored?

Do you have hope that they can be restored? Why or why not?

In Scripture, we clearly see that God is devoted to peace and reconciliation. From the moment Eve and then Adam took a bite of the fruit of the Tree of Knowledge of Good and Evil and humankind was separated from God by sin, God began His work to restore His relationship with us.

Read the following verses. What does each have to say about God's desire for reconciliation?

Isaiah 53:5

John 1:29

> There is something about a once-majestic old house that calls out for restoration. . . . Often there are relationships in our lives that are like old houses. . . . But there is hope for these relationships, for our God is one who desires restoration and reconciliation.

2 Corinthians 5:18-20

Ephesians 2:18

Colossians 1:19-20

Though humankind broke fellowship with God through sinful actions, God desires reconciliation—a restored harmony—in our relationship with Him and sent Jesus to carry out that reconciliation. Romans 5:1 says, "Therefore, having been justified through faith, we have peace with God through our LORD Jesus" (NKJV). Through Jesus' sacrifice, we are right with God.

As we see in Scripture, God is devoted to reconciliation and restoration of relationships. Do you think you've shared this view as it relates to your relationships? If so, how? If not, why?

On an everyday, practical level, do you practice restoration in your relationships? What might that look like? Give some specific examples.

Because reconciliation is so important to God, He wants it to be important to us as well. In Matthew 5:23-24 Jesus says, "Therefore, if you bring your gift to the altar and there remember that your brother or sister has something against you, leave your gift at the altar and go. First make things right with your brother or sister and then come back and offer your gift." We will focus on this verse tomorrow, but for now, consider how it speaks to you.

What does this verse mean to you? Why do you think Jesus says to reconcile with one another before bringing your offering to God?

Because reconciliation is so important to God, He wants it to be important to us as well.

89

Has there ever been a time in your life when you felt God calling you to seek reconciliation with another person? How did you respond? How did the other person respond?

Sometimes our efforts at reconciliation can inspire others and lead them to their own healing. How does Anna's physical restoration of her parents' home into the Inn at Shining Waters affect others in the story?

Sometimes our efforts at reconciliation can inspire others and lead them to their own healing.

Much like the act of forgiveness, reconciliation and restoration must be practiced, and practiced often, in our relationships. How might God be calling you to practice reconciliation today?

Talk to God

Loving God, thank you that you are a God of reconciliation, that you want to be in a harmonious, intimate relationship with me, and that you are always willing and eager to make that happen. Allow me the grace to offer restoration to others, and help me to have a willing and forgiving spirit. Give me the strength to humble myself and ask for forgiveness from others. Amen.

As You Go

Though the work may be hard and the task grueling, great beauty comes out of restoration. How have you seen God make beautiful things out of ruins? Do you recognize God doing that in your life right now? How?

DAY 2: DISCOVERING FREEDOM IN RESTORATION

Read God's Word

Therefore, if you bring your gift to the altar and there remember that your brother or sister has something against you, leave your gift at the altar and go. First make things right with your brother or sister and then come back and offer your gift.

Matthew 5:23-24

Reflect and Respond

Restoring a house takes considerable effort, and it certainly takes time. The transformation doesn't come all at once, but slowly, bit by bit, plank by plank. Just as choosing to forgive someone can be a process, filled with stops and starts and twists and turns, so choosing to seek restoration in a relationship can be slow and requires loads of patience.

Yet as we read in the verses for today from Matthew 5:23-24, God values reconciliation and even commands it. God calls us to respond in obedience and work to restore those important relationships in our lives.

How do you feel about God's command to "make things right with your brother or sister" (v. 24)? What emotions does that command stir within you?

So, why do it? Why put ourselves through all the work and heartache that comes with reconciling troubled relationships? What if the relationship was never all that great to begin with?

Anna and her mother-in-law had a difficult relationship from the start, yet Anna determines to forgive her and makes a connection with Eunice, treating her with kindness and respect.

Why do you think Anna was so determined to have a good relationship with Eunice, even after all Eunice put her through? How do you think you would have responded in Anna's situation?

> Just as choosing to forgive someone can be a process, filled with stops and starts and twists and turns, so choosing to seek restoration in a relationship can be slow and requires loads of patience.

Deep down, our hearts desire restoration because it gives our earth-bound bodies a reminder of heaven and of a complete and perfect relationship with the only One who can make that happen. Though our relationships this side of heaven will never be perfect no matter how much we try, they are a gift nonetheless. We were made for relationship, and those relationships can reflect the glory and love of the One who made us and redeems us. God works through us and through our relationships with one another to give us glimpses of His perfect love: "The LORD works righteousness; does justice for all who are oppressed. . . . The LORD is compassionate and merciful, very patient, and full of faithful love" (Psalm 103:6, 8).

In these verses from Psalm 103, which characteristic of God do you most connect with today and why?

Excerpt from *River's Call,* Chapter 24

"I never had a chance to learn too much about Adam's upbringing," [Anna said to Eunice.] "I know his father died when he was younger. And from what I heard, it seemed you spent quite a bit of time and energy on him. Weren't you two rather close?"

Eunice seemed to soften now. "We were close. Adam was my right hand after his father passed. I depended on him for everything. He was my—my best friend." Her voice broke slightly.

Anna leaned forward. "He was a good man, Eunice. You must've done a good job raising him."

Eunice looked truly surprised. "You truly think so?"

Anna nodded. "Oh, he was a bit spoiled. But you expect that with an only child. I was a little spoiled too."

Eunice blinked. "You?"

"In some ways, I was. But I was also a hard worker. And Adam was a hard worker too. But he also knew how to play. I think one of the things that drew me to him was his sense of fun and adventure. He was always so full of life and fun. That was very attractive."

"Yes," Eunice said eagerly. "He was full of life, wasn't he?"

"I sometimes wonder what it would've been like if he hadn't been hurt like that . . . in the war."

Eunice nodded sadly. "I do too. He never should've been in active service. He wasn't like that. He'd never been the sort of boy to play with guns or roughhouse like some boys. I remember how he tried to rescue a bird that flew into the picture window, putting it in a box with a tea towel, hoping that it would live . . . how he cried when it didn't." She sniffed. "He was too tenderhearted to march with a gun."

"And yet he seemed eager to go." Anna remembered her dismay when he'd been so enthusiastic to join his buddies and head off to war.

"That was his devil-may-care side... he loved adventures and had no idea what the war would really be like."

"He found out quickly." Anna tried not to remember the look in his blue eyes when he returned to them... as if the light had gone out.

Eunice was crying now, sitting by herself on the strangely shaped sofa and wiping her eyes. Anna went over and sat next to her, wrapping an arm around the frail shoulders. "I wish we could've been friends," Anna confessed. "All those years when we were both suffering.... I wish we'd known that we both missed him."

Eunice nodded then quietly blew her nose. "I always blamed you, Anna," she whispered. "I felt you stole him from me... and then he never came back."

"The war took him from both of us."

"Yes... I think you are right."

Now they just sat there for a long moment and then Eunice stiffened, squared her shoulders, and said it was time for bed. Anna stood, offering her a hand to help her up.

Eunice paused after she stood, looking intently at Anna. "I have found that anger and bitterness become rather cumbersome... the older I get."

"It's better to just set those things aside."

"Yes... I suppose so."

Anna walked her through the house, going through the kitchen and to the back door. "It's dark out, Eunice, do you mind if I walk you home?"

Eunice looked surprised and then relieved. "If you'd like."

Anna smiled at her. "I would."

• • • • • • •

In Micah 6:8 we read, "He has told you, O man, what is good; and what does the LORD require of you but to do justice, to love kindness, and to walk humbly with your God?"

We are told to "do justice" and "love kindness." Do those two actions seem compatible to you, or do they seem to oppose one another? Why do you think they are included together in this verse?

How did Anna "love kindness" when it came to her relationship with Eunice?

"Anna went over and sat next to [Eunice], wrapping an arm around the frail shoulders. 'I wish we could've been friends,' Anna confessed.' 'All those years when we were both suffering .... I wish we'd known that we both missed him.'"

When we finally learn the root of Eunice's bitterness toward Anna, it seems a shame that she has let those poisonous emotions affect her life. How has bitterness and lack of reconciliation affected Eunice's life?

How has it affected others in her life, such as Lauren?

Talk to God

Lord, give me the strength to practice kindness, patience, and love in my relationships. Help me to know when to speak and give me the words to say to foster reconciliation and restoration. I want to reflect your light to others and to remind them of how good you are. Thank you for your unending love and patience with me. Amen.

As You Go

Is there a relationship in your life that needs restoration? What do you feel when you think about that person and the circumstances surrounding your relationship? How is God calling you to "love kindness" in your situation? Do something today to take a step toward reconciliation.

DAY 3: POINTING OTHERS TOWARD THE GREAT RESTORER

Read God's Word

Jesus told them this parable: "Suppose someone among you had one hundred sheep and lost one of them. Wouldn't he leave the other ninety-nine in the pasture and search for the lost one until he finds it? And when he finds it, he is thrilled and places it on his shoulders. When he arrives home, he calls together his friends and neighbors, saying to them, 'Celebrate with me because I've found my lost sheep.' In the same way, I tell you, there will be more joy in heaven over one sinner who changes both heart and life than over ninety-nine righteous people who have no need to change their hearts and lives."

Luke 15:3-7

Reflect and Respond

Though our hearts long for perfection and comfort, we live in a fallen world where there is pain and hardship and judgment. All of us make mistakes daily, with varying consequences—some of which can be life changing.

When Lauren discovers she is pregnant, she is devastated and sure that her life is ruined. Fearing judgment and public shame, Eunice convinces Lauren and Donald to get married quickly, even though the foundation of their relationship is shaky at best.

What do you think might have happened to Lauren if she hadn't gotten pregnant? Do you think her life would have taken a different trajectory? Why or why not?

Is there a circumstance in your life or a choice that you've made that you feel has defined you? What is it, and how has it affected you?

Like most of us, Lauren just wanted security, protection, and comfort, but the desperate search for those things began to define her life. And when she couldn't find those things in her marriage, she began to spiral out of control, desperate for something to numb the pain. Lost and confused, she felt that she couldn't be saved and turned from those who wanted to help her.

But Anna never gave up on Lauren, and God doesn't give up on us either.

Today's Scripture passage from the Gospel of Luke, often called The Parable of the Lost Sheep, is a beautiful picture of how God takes great pleasure in bringing someone who is lost into His care. Though we may run and turn from him, God continues to pursue us, eager to bring our hungry spirits home to Him. And when God finds us, weary and afraid to come home, He does not leave us but puts us on his shoulders and carries us to safety.

I remember a particularly difficult time a number of years ago shortly after my older son entered into treatment for schizophrenia. I was busy taking him to lots of appointments, regulating his medications, trying to get him back to a healthy place while still keeping up with my contracted writing projects. It was very stressful, and it felt as if our whole family was being tested and tried on every level—a truly dark and frightening era. But in the midst of what sometimes felt like chaos, I could still sense God's love. Although I didn't know what the outcome would be and was filled with questions, I knew I was in God's hands and that He was taking care of us.

> Even when it seems that we are hopelessly lost, disoriented, and wounded by our bad choices and the judgments of others, God does not give up on us but chooses to restore and renew.

Has there ever been a time in your life when you've felt lost, isolated, and abandoned? What were the circumstances?

How did God meet you in that place?

Even when it seems that we are hopelessly lost, disoriented, and wounded by our bad choices and the judgments of others, God does not give up on us but chooses to restore and renew. Not only does God rescue us; God transforms us. God said,

I will give them an undivided heart and put a new spirit in them; I will remove from them their heart of stone and give them a heart of flesh. Then they will follow my decrees and be careful to keep my laws. They will be my people, and I will be their God.

Ezekiel 11:19-20 NIV

For those of us who believe, God has claimed us as His. Left to our own devices, our hearts can be divided—pulled this way and that by our own selfish desires and the pressures of this world. But God pledges to give us an undivided heart—one that longs for God.

Read Mark 4:1-20. Based on this passage from Mark, what do you think the prophet Ezekiel meant by "heart of stone"?

What does 2 Corinthians 5:17 say about how God transforms us?

Is this promise easy or hard for you to believe? Why?

Are you claiming this promise in your life right now? If not, what is holding you back?

Do you know someone who is lost, wandering aimlessly and losing hope? What words are you speaking to this person—words of judgment and shame or words of hope?

How can you remind this person of God's promises to rescue and restore?

Left to our own devices, our hearts can be divided–pulled this way and that by our own selfish desires and the pressures of this world. But God pledges to give us an undivided heart–one that longs for God.

Talk to God

God, thank you for running after me and pursuing me, even though I sometimes turn from you. When I am discouraged, help me to know that you have promised to give me a renewed spirit and that you do not leave me to figure all this out on my own. Help me to speak words of life and encouragement to those who are lost and hurting, and to hold back my words of judgment. Help me to remind others that you are the Great Rescuer and that we can put our hope securely in you. Amen.

As You Go

Though Lauren's unplanned pregnancy changed her life, the whole family was ultimately blessed by the arrival of little Sarah. How have you witnessed or experienced God's blessings in the midst of seemingly devastating circumstances? Give thanks for these blessings today.

DAY 4: PADDLING OUR CANOES

Read God's Word

The wise in heart are called discerning, and gracious words promote instruction.
Proverbs 16:21 NIV

Don't let any foul words come out of your mouth. Only say what is helpful when it is needed for building up the community so that it benefits those who hear what you say.
Ephesians 4:29

Your speech should always be gracious and sprinkled with insight so that you may know how to respond to every person.

Colossians 4:6

Reflect and Respond

The Inn at Shining Waters Series revolves around a cast of women whose lives are inextricably woven together. The dynamics of these relationships—mothers and daughters, through both blood and marriage—are complicated and often difficult to navigate.

Consider the relationships between the characters listed below. Using a few words or phrases, how would you describe each relationship?

Anna and Lauren

Anna and Hazel

Anna and Eunice

Eunice and Lauren

Lauren and Sarah

Anna and Sarah

Which of these relationships do you most identify with and why?

Because the relationships with the women in our lives are important and enduring, they are worth the time and effort it takes to make them strong. And as we see with Anna and Eunice, spoken words play an important part in our relationships with other women.

Today's Scripture passages give us wisdom about how our speech affects one another. When our words are filled with grace, others are able to hear and learn. We are to speak words that build up, not tear down, and that benefit those who are listening. Our words are to be gracious and kind, and filled with insight.

Take some time to think about how your words affect the women in your life. What words do you speak well? In what areas might you need to reconsider your words?

Anna often holds her tongue when it comes to speaking her opinion or judgment of others. Do you admire this about her, or do you think she's too timid? Why?

> Spoken words play an important part in our relationships with other women. . . . When our words are filled with grace, others are able to hear and learn.

When Anna learns that Lauren is having a hard time taking care of the new baby and keeping up a household, Anna decides to visit and help Lauren get through a rough time. But when she gets to Lauren's house, Anna is disappointed to find that Lauren has given up and is moving in with Eunice, lured back by the promise of a full-time nanny and housekeeper and an "easier" life. Anna is disheartened by this turn of events, but Clark encourages her that she has to let go and let Lauren live her own life.

Excerpt from *River's Call,* Chapter 19

"Lauren has you as an example, Anna," Clark said. "Eventually she's going to figure things out. But maybe it's going to take some time."

Anna considered this. "Maybe you're right. But it feels painful just the same. I had hoped for so much more for Lauren."

"You know what your grandmother would say, Anna."

She took in a long deep breath and slowly let it out. "That Lauren must paddle her own canoe."

"And right now, Lauren is just taking the easy route, going downstream with the flow of the water.

"That's true enough. But the easy route can easily wind up in rapids or a waterfall."

He nodded. "And maybe that will be her wake-up call. In the meantime, it doesn't seem there's much you can do."

• • • • • • •

Have you ever had to let someone "paddle his or her own canoe"? How did that feel? What was the outcome of the situation?

Proverbs 2:2 beckons us to "Turn your ear toward wisdom, and stretch your mind toward understanding." But often we are so caught up in our own plans and perspective that we fail to heed the warning signs and words of caution from those who love us.

Have you ever failed to listen and paddled your own canoe into trouble? What happened?

How can you speak words of healing, love, and encouragement to someone in your life who is paddling her own canoe?

Talk to God

God, I pray for guidance and understanding as I approach these important relationships with the women in my life. I pray for eyes to see where they are hurting and ears to listen to the cries of their hearts. I pray for lips that should sometimes be silent, and a tongue that speaks words of life and healing. Give me wisdom and understanding, Lord, and help us to point each other back to you. Amen.

As You Go

Reflect on the following questions today: In what ways has your relationship with your mother (or mother-in-law) affected and influenced you? How do you wish it were different, or better? Do you have daughters (or daughters-in-law)? How might you consider improving your relationship with them?

DAY 5: BESTOWING A BLESSING

Read God's Word

The LORD said to Abram, "Leave your land, your family, and your father's household for the land that I will show you.

I will make of you a great nation and will bless you. I will make your name respected, and you will be a blessing. I will bless those who bless you, those who curse you I will curse; all the families of earth will be blessed because of you.

Abram left just as the LORD told him, and Lot went with him. Now Abram was 75 years old when he left Haran. Abram took his wife Sarai, his nephew Lot, all of their possessions, and those who became members of their household in Haran; and they set out for the land of Canaan. . . . The LORD appeared to Abram and said, "I give this land to your descendants," so Abram built an altar there to the LORD who appeared to him. . . .

The LORD's word came to Abram in a vision, "Don't be afraid, Abram. I am your protector. Your reward will be very great."

But Abram said, "LORD God, what can you possibly give me, since I still have no children? The head of my household is Eliezer, a man from Damascus." He continued, "Since you haven't given me any children, the head of my household will be my heir."

The LORD's word came immediately to him, "This man will not be your heir. Your heir will definitely be your very own biological child."

Then he brought Abram outside and said, "Look up at the sky and count the stars if you think you can count them." He continued, "This is how many children you will have." Abram trusted the LORD.

Genesis 12:1-2, 4-7; 15:1-6

Reflect and Respond

The nation of Israel's history began with a blessing to Abraham. God said, "All the families of earth will be blessed because of you" (Genesis 12:3). And so Abraham (at that point called Abram) was blessed—that is, he was granted God's favor. In the Greek and Hebrew, to be "blessed" suggests that one is under God's divine protection, and that protection can be counted on and trusted, as God is the giver of everything good and pure.

As we see in Scripture, blessings were often given as a public declaration of God's favor on a person. Men blessed their wives and children (see Genesis 27:27-29), and rulers blessed their subjects (see 2 Samuel 6:18). And while the Old Testament blessings were more focused on wealth and prosperity, the New Testament declares the importance of the spiritual blessings we have received through our faith in Jesus Christ.

Read Galatians 3:8-14. How has God's pledge that "all the families of the earth will be blessed" (from Genesis 12:3) been fulfilled through Jesus?

What do Galatians 3:3 and Romans 4:6-9 tell us about how we have been blessed through Jesus?

> In the Greek and Hebrew, to be "blessed" suggests that one is under God's divine protection, and that protection can be counted on and trusted.

From the moment Anna sees baby Sarah and then holds her in her arms, Anna feels a special connection to her tiny granddaughter, and speaks a blessing over her.

Excerpt from *River's Call,* Chapter 13

"Oh, sweet Sarah." Anna gazed into the baby's slate-blue eyes. They reminded her of deep pools along the river. "You are a beautiful little princess. A Siuslaw princess," she whispered. "The blood of your ancestors flows through you. I pray it's a blessing....

"You'll come to visit me on the river," she said quietly, "you'll learn to use a canoe and to fish and maybe you'll even weave a basket or two.... You have spirit," Anna told her. "You will grow up to be someone very special, Sarah Pearl. I just know it. You will be our little Siuslaw princess....

"You will have to be very strong," Anna whispered. "Not everyone will love you like I do. But you have your ancestors' blood, your great-great-grandmother's blood, and that will make you strong. I can feel your spirit, little one. You will be very strong." She leaned over and kissed the top of Sarah's head. "Be blessed, little Siuslaw princess. Be very, very blessed."

· · · · · · ·

Ephesians 1:3 says that God "has blessed us in Christ with every spiritual blessing that comes from heaven." Because we have received God's blessings through Christ, we are called to bless others in return.

What do you think it means to "bless" someone? Can you bless someone through words, actions, or both? Give some examples.

Have you ever received a verbal blessing from someone? How did it affect you?

> Because we have received God's blessings through Christ, we are called to bless others in return.

As we've already discussed, our words have great power to affect the people in our lives. Is there someone in your life who would benefit from a verbal or written blessing from you? How is God leading you to speak a blessing to that person today?

Scripture also tells us that blessings should be given to those who oppose and mistreat us. Read Luke 6:27-28. What might it mean to bless someone who curses you? What would that look like?

Why do you think Jesus would command this?

How does Anna strive to bless those who "curse" her? What can you learn from her example?

Read the following passage and circle the words that describe those whom Jesus says are blessed.

Now when Jesus saw the crowds, he went up on a mountainside and sat down. His
disciples came to him, and he began to teach them. He said:
"Blessed are the poor in spirit, for theirs is the kingdom of heaven.
Blessed are those who mourn, for they will be comforted.
Blessed are the meek, for they will inherit the earth.
Blessed are those who hunger and thirst for righteousness, for they will be filled.
Blessed are the merciful, for they will be shown mercy.
Blessed are the pure in heart, for they will see God.
Blessed are the peacemakers, for they will be called children of God.
Blessed are those who are persecuted because of righteousness, for theirs is the
kingdom of heaven.
Blessed are you when people insult you, persecute you and falsely say all kinds of
evil against you because of me."

Matthew 5:1-11 NIV

Which of the characteristics that you circled do you most identify with today?

How does hearing God's blessing renew your hope and give you strength?

Talk to God

Lord God, I praise you and thank you for the blessing that you have so graciously bestowed upon me—that you call me your own and promise to work good in my life. Help me to live out that blessing by trusting in you daily and speaking that light and blessing into the lives of others. Give me patience and grace to bless those who hurt me, and give me strength to remember your promises. Amen.

As You Go

How might you give an intentional blessing to someone in your life? Consider writing out a special blessing to give to a child, spouse, or friend. Take the time to present it to the person as a special gift. After delivering the blessing, journal about the experience (journaling pages are provided at the back of the book).

VIDEO NOTES
A FEW MINUTES WITH MELODY

INTERESTING INSIGHTS:

POINTS I'D LIKE TO DISCUSS WITH THE GROUP:

WEEK 5
THE VALUE OF COMMUNITY

Scripture for the Week

*You divine messengers,
bless the LORD!
You who are mighty in power
and keep his word,
who obey everything he says,
bless him!*
Psalm 103:20

Excerpt from *River's Call,* Chapter 16

The trip [back to the river] took a couple hours longer than the trip out had taken. But with numerous stops to tend to the baby, tend to Lauren, it was mid-afternoon by the time Anna parked the car in town. "Clark is meeting us with the boat," she explained. "It's faster than the back road, not to mention smoother." She glanced up at the sky. "And it's a perfect day for the river. But let's bundle Sarah up just the same."

Anna held the baby as Clark guided the boat up the river. Lauren, to Anna's delight, seemed to be happy just to sit and look at the scenery, occasionally commenting on how beautiful everything was. "I forgot how pretty it is here, Mom," she said happily.

Anna smiled. It was the first time Lauren had sounded happy in days.

As the boat made its way up the Siuslaw, Anna talked quietly to the baby, telling her about the river, about the fish and the birds, about how one day Sarah would paddle her own canoe around the shining waters. "Just like a real Siuslaw princess," she promised as the inn came into sight.

"Everything looks so nice," Lauren told Anna. "The flowers blooming, the picnic tables—and you even got more boats. It's like a real resort."

Anna laughed. "And you used to think it was the last resort."

"You ladies go in and get settled," Clark said as he tied the boat to the dock then gave them each a hand getting out. "Marshall and I will get all this stuff unloaded."

They were just going up the dock when Babette and Hazel came down to meet them. "Allo, allo," Babette called out.

"Welcome home," Hazel said heartily. Then both the older women oohed and

aahed over the baby.

"She ees so beautiful," Babette gushed. "She ees so much like Anna when she was a petite bebe."

Lauren nodded as she looked down at her baby, still in Anna's arms. "Everyone thinks she takes after Mom."

"Eet ees a good thing," Babette told her.

"A very good thing." Hazel put her arm around Anna's shoulders and squeezed her. "We're so glad you're back."

"And I have saved lunch for you," Babette said. "If you are hungry."

"I'm starving," Lauren told her. "And Mom says you're going to teach me how to cook French food."

"I am pleased to teach you." Babette grabbed Lauren's hand, swinging it as they walked to the house. "Just the way I teach your mama."

· · · · · · ·

Day 1: We Were Not Meant to Be Alone

Read God's Word

On the day the LORD God made earth and sky—before any wild plants appeared on the earth, and before any field crops grew, because the LORD God hadn't yet sent rain on the earth and there was still no human being to farm the fertile land, though a stream rose from the earth and watered all of the fertile land—the LORD God formed the human from the topsoil of the fertile land and blew life's breath into his nostrils. The human came to life. . . .

The LORD God took the human and settled him in the garden of Eden to farm it and to take care of it. . . . Then the LORD God said, "It's not good that the human is alone. I will make him a helper that is perfect for him." So the LORD God formed from the fertile land all the wild animals and all the birds in the sky and brought them to the human to see what he would name them. The human gave each living being its name. The human named all the livestock, all the birds in the sky, and all the wild animals. But a helper perfect for him was nowhere to be found.

So the LORD God put the human into a deep and heavy sleep, and took one of his ribs and closed up the flesh over it. With the rib taken from the human, the LORD God fashioned a woman and brought her to the human being.

Genesis 2:4-7, 15, 18-22

Reflect and Respond

From the moment God created man, God knew that man shouldn't live alone. God brought Adam all the animals he had created, and Adam named them and cared for them. But they were not enough—Adam needed a match, a "helper" to live life with. He needed someone he could talk to, someone he could connect with, someone he could love.

We were not meant to live in isolation. We were created in the image of a relational God, and we were meant to connect with and share our lives with other human beings. To live in community with others is a gift, and one that we should wholeheartedly embrace.

For me, community begins at home. I realize it's not like that for everyone, but I'm blessed with a husband who is also my best friend. And I realize that's a relationship that deserves my time and nurturing. Also, because I grew up in a strong extended family, I respect my relationships with my relatives and consider them part of my tribe. Beyond that, I try to let God lead me, and there have been numerous times when I've felt a God-nudge to "adopt" a friend as a "sister." I do not take this kind of nudge lightly, and when it happens I realize that this means I'm committing my friendship through the good, the bad, and the in between. But it always ends up being a blessing—on both sides—and I do not regret it.

Do you have a strong community—a "tribe" of people who love and care about you and in whose lives you are invested? Who are they?

Has there ever been a time in your life when you didn't have community? What was that time like?

Read Ecclesiastes 4:9-10. Describe a time in your life when your community was there to pick you up when you fell. What was it like to know that others were there for you when you needed them?

> We were created in the image of a relational God, and we were meant to connect with and share our lives with other human beings. To live in community with others is a gift, and one that we should wholeheartedly embrace.

Community comes to us in different forms. Sometimes it's in the form of a new friendship that is so natural it seems as though you've known the person your whole life. Sometimes it happens among those who know you best—your parents, siblings, and childhood friends. It can happen randomly and unexpectedly, and when it happens so easily and naturally, we feel very blessed and grateful to experience it.

But there are also times when community doesn't come all that easily. When the church small group you were placed in seems filled with people you have nothing in common with. When your move to a new city has left you feeling lonely and vulnerable. When your sister, who you've been trying to spend more time with, is pushing all your buttons and driving you crazy. But even in difficult and awkward relationships, God can bring about beauty and bless us with community.

> Even in difficult and awkward relationships, God can bring about beauty and bless us with community.

In The Inn at Shining Waters Series, there are some characters that seem to instantly bond and develop deep community with one another. List a few of these relationships and why you think they work so well or what you admire about their relationships.

Some characters—such as Anna and Lauren—have difficult relationships but, through time and effort, experience beautiful transformation in their relationships. Are you experiencing any difficult relationships in your community? Do you have hope that time and effort may turn those relationships around?

What is your view on community? Have you valued it and invested in it over the years? If so, how? If not, what has been holding you back?

Talk to God

Dear God, thank you that you created us for community and that you anticipate our needs by filling our lives with others who can care for us and love us—and for whom we can do that in return. When it is difficult to live with others in community, help me to remember the blessing that it brings. And when the moments in community are sweet, may I praise you for all your good gifts. Amen.

As You Go

Read Galatians 5:14: "The entire law is summed up in a single command: 'Love your neighbor as yourself'" (NIV). Reflect today about how you view community in your life. Are you living out this command?

DAY 2: MANY PLAYERS, MANY PARTS

Read God's Word

There should be no division in the body, but that its parts should have equal concern for each other. If one part suffers, every part suffers with it; if one part is honored, every part rejoices with it. Now you are the body of Christ, and each one of you is a part of it.

1 Corinthians 12:25-27 NIV

In the same way, though there are many of us, we are one body in Christ, and individually we belong to each other.

Romans 12:5

Reflect and Respond

Community is defined as "a unified body of individuals; a group of people with a common interest." An inspiring example of community occurs every few years as the world readies for the Olympic games. In our country alone, thousands of athletes, who normally compete against each other for titles and accolades, come together to be a part of one team with one goal. They are unified under the flag of the United States of America, and they are committed to representing their country well.

As believers, we are unified as the body of Christ. Though each of us comes to the table with different personalities, strengths, and weaknesses, we are on the same team. We have the same goal. We are one in Christ.

Today's Scripture passages from the Apostle Paul's first letter to the Corinthians and his letter to the Romans teach that there is to be no division in the body of Christ. Both passages emphasize the same point: since we are united in the body of Christ, we are connected to one another. Romans 12:5 even says we "belong to each other."

> As believers, we are unified as the body of Christ. Though each of us comes to the table with different personalities, strengths, and weaknesses, we are on the same team. We have the same goal. We are one in Christ.

111

Have you ever thought about other believers this way—that you belong to each other? What do you think today's Scripture verses are implying about how we should live in community and how we should treat one another?

It has been said that being in a church is like being in a family—you don't necessarily get to choose who is in your family, and you may have little in common with them, but you are obligated and committed to one another in Christ. Have you ever considered your community in this light? How do today's Scripture verses challenge you to reexamine your view of your community?

We should encourage one another to devote ourselves to our gifts, cultivating and celebrating those things that only we can do.

Though we are one unified body, God has given each of us gifts and talents that are unique and essential. In Romans 12:4-8 we read,

> *We have many parts in one body, but the parts don't all have the same function. In the same way, though there are many of us, we are one body in Christ, and individually we belong to each other. We have different gifts that are consistent with God's grace that has been given to us. If your gift is prophecy, you should prophesy in proportion to your faith. If your gift is service, devote yourself to serving. If your gift is teaching, devote yourself to teaching. If your gift is encouragement, devote yourself to encouraging. The one giving should do it with no strings attached. The leader should lead with passion. The one showing mercy should be cheerful.*

As members of a community, we should strive to both encourage and utilize the gifts of our members. Whether it's preaching a sermon or loving on the babies in the nursery, each gift is of equal importance and necessity as we demonstrate the love of God to others. And, as this passage in Romans says, we should encourage one another to devote ourselves to our gifts, cultivating and using and celebrating those things that only we can do. Much like Hazel did for Anna, we should champion each other in our gifts. When we see strengths and talents in our friends and family, we should be quick to acknowledge those and to celebrate how God has made them unique individuals.

It required a full cast of friends to help Anna heal and take a proactive role in her own life. From what you have read thus far, which relationships do you think have been most valuable to Anna, and why?

Has there been a time in your life when someone has helped foster and encourage your strengths? What happened, and what effect did that person's encouragement have on you?

Read 1 Peter 4:10. In what areas do you think God has gifted you? What are your strengths? What tasks, causes, or opportunities light up your spirit and excite you?

Are you actively using your gifts in your community? If so, how? If not, what's holding you back?

Talk to God

Lord, I praise you for your creativity. Though you have given us varied talents and strengths, you also have blessed us with one heart that is devoted to you. Help me to celebrate the various gifts I see in those around me, and to encourage and affirm them. Give me the courage to use my own talents and to not be afraid to celebrate them because they came from you. Amen.

As You Go

Today, pray that God would open your eyes to focus on the strengths and talents of those around you, and make a conscious effort to encourage and affirm others in their gifts.

DAY 3: THE ESSENTIALS OF LIVING IN COMMUNITY

Read God's Word

I appeal to you, brothers and sisters, in the name of our LORD Jesus Christ, that all of you agree with one another in what you say and that there be no divisions among you, but that you be perfectly united in mind and thought.

1 Corinthians 1:10 NIV

Reflect and Respond

Sharing our lives with others requires us to go against our natural inclinations and to choose, in thought and action, to put the needs of others ahead of our own, to love harmony, and to open ourselves up to be vulnerable and authentic.

Living in community is, as the Apostle Paul describes, being united in mind and thought. Although immensely rewarding and fulfilling, choosing to live in community—*with no divisions*—doesn't tend to happen easily or naturally. We were made to be in community, and our hearts long to be connected with others, but often our fears and our desire for self-protection hold us back from truly experiencing the fullness that comes when we live with others in community.

Sharing our lives with others requires us to go against our natural inclinations and to choose, in thought and action, to put the needs of others ahead of our own, to love harmony, and to open ourselves up to be vulnerable and authentic.

See what the following Scriptures have to say about living in community with other believers. What does each instruct us to do? The first, which is today's Scripture verse, is done for you.

1 Corinthians 1:10
Get along with one another; be like-minded.

Philippians 2:3

James 5:16

Hebrews 10:24

Which of the things commanded in these verses are most difficult for you to live out?

How can you challenge your natural inclinations in order to open yourself up to your community?

Are you giving your best to the most important people in your life? Are you blessing them, first and foremost, with your strengths and gifts?

Though living in community can be downright difficult sometimes, the blessings found in these relationships can be life changing and pivotal, challenging us in the best of ways. When Anna first returns home to the river, she is broken and downtrodden from years of enduring her mother-in-law's abuse. She has given up hope for a different life. But when she meets Hazel, all that changes. Hazel affirms Anna's heritage and her gifts of hospitality and fosters Anna's dream of creating an inn out of her parents' property. Because of Hazel's encouragement, enthusiasm, and love, Anna is finally able to realize her potential and live into her gifts.

Hebrews 10:24 urges us to "spur one another on toward love and good deeds" (NIV). To spur means to "urge and incite into action." Taken literally, it means to poke someone in the side, as you would a horse. Do you practice giving this kind of encouragement to those in your community? Is there a dream or a goal that you can help someone achieve? Make a few notes about how you might act for that person's benefit.

Each of us is on a journey, fraught with highs and lows and perils along the way. When we are afraid to let others into our lives, to let them know where we are struggling and hurting, we suffer alone.

Anna suffered in silence for many years, saying nothing in response to Eunice's criticisms and insults. Though the words wounded her deeply, she never let on how the words affected her or shared her pain with anyone. But when Hazel witnesses Eunice's words in action for the first time, she quickly jumps to Anna's defense.

> Though living in community can be downright sometimes, the blessings found in these relationships can be life changing and pivotal, challenging us in the best of ways.

115

Excerpt from *River's Call,* Chapter 8

"Oh, Lauren, you are missing all the fun," Eunice called out in a snide tone. "Your mother plans to teach you to weave Indian baskets and turn your baby into a papoose. In no time, I expect to see you wearing moccasins and beads, dear. Can you imagine?"

"What?" Lauren looked at Anna in confusion.

"Oh, your grandmother is just being humorous." Anna felt an old familiar flush of anger and humiliation running through her as she went over to the sink. All the times that Eunice had made fun of her came rushing back—how had she endured those years? And did she have to continue to endure it, right here in her own home?

"I do not find any of that to be humorous," Hazel said stiffly. "In fact, I find it to be rather bad taste, Eunice. And I think you owe Anna an apology."

"You expect me to apologize?" Eunice sounded affronted.

"You have insulted your hostess," Hazel continued. "I'm not sure how you were raised, Eunice, but I was taught to be more respectful than that. Especially when staying as a guest in someone's home."

"Oh, don't be too shocked, Hazel." Lauren went over and put an arm around Anna. "Grandmother is always like that. But you're used to it, aren't you, Mom?"

Anna turned and looked at Lauren. "I suppose I am used to it, Lauren. In the same way that a dog that is regularly beaten becomes used to it. It still hurts."

Lauren looked surprised. "Really?"

Anna just nodded then returned to rinsing dishes.

"Then I agree with Hazel, Grandmother. I think you owe my mother an apology."

"Well!" Eunice made a harrumph and Anna heard the sound of a chair scraping across the floor. "Excuse me!" The sound of footsteps was followed by the firm closing of the front door.

"Was that supposed to be an apology?" Hazel asked.

"Maybe for Grandmother it was," Lauren said.

Anna looked back at Lauren and smiled. "You know, sweetie, that is the first time you've ever stood up for me."

"Really?" Lauren looked sad. "I guess I never knew that it bothered you so much."

"You never knew?" Anna frowned.

"You always seemed so strong, Mom, like nothing could penetrate or hurt you."

Anna just shook her head. "I guess I put on a good act then. But all those words, all those years . . . they hurt. Trust me—they hurt a lot. They still do."

Lauren seemed truly surprised. "I'm sorry, Mom. I really didn't know."

Anna reached out and hugged Lauren. "Maybe that's my fault . . . for keeping my feelings locked up all those years."

· · · · · ·

Until Anna revealed the pain that Eunice's verbal abuse had caused her, Lauren didn't know that her mother had needed an ally and an advocate all those years to defend or fight for her. A big part of being in community is learning to fight for one another, to use the light of Christ to push back the darkness of this world. But when we refuse to let others in, appearing to be strong and holding it all together, we hinder others from really knowing our struggles and coming alongside us to fight for truth to rule in our lives.

How does James 5:16 instruct us to fight for one another?

Is this a new concept for you—that we need to fight for one another? Is there someone in your life right now who is fighting a battle? What are some ways that you can fight with her or him?

Galatians 6:2 says, "Carry each other's burdens and so you will fulfill the law of Christ." How can you open yourself up and invite others to help carry your burdens?

> A big part of being in community is learning to fight for one another, to use the light of Christ to push back the darkness of this world.

Talk to God

Jesus, you are the light of the world, and the darkness stands no chance against you. Give me eyes to see those around me who are fighting tough battles, and help me to fight with them. Help me to open my heart and my life up to others so they will know how to fight for me as well. I don't have to be strong, Lord, for you are my strength. Thank you for your love and protection. Amen.

As You Go

Psalm 103:20 calls those of us who put our hope in the LORD "you divine messengers." Is there a person to whom God is calling you to be a "divine messenger"? Pray about this today.

DAY 4: GO AND DO

Read God's Word

A legal expert stood up to test Jesus. "Teacher," he said, "what must I do to gain eternal life?"

Jesus replied, "What is written in the Law? How do you interpret it?"

He responded, "You must love the LORD your God with all your heart, with all your being, with all your strength, and with all your mind, and love your neighbor as yourself."

Jesus said to him, "You have answered correctly. Do this and you will live."

But the legal expert wanted to prove that he was right, so he said to Jesus, "And who is my neighbor?"

Jesus replied, "A man went down from Jerusalem to Jericho. He encountered thieves, who stripped him naked, beat him up, and left him near death. Now it just so happened that a priest was also going down the same road. When he saw the injured man, he crossed over to the other side of the road and went on his way. Likewise, a Levite came by that spot, saw the injured man, and crossed over to the other side of the road and went on his way. A Samaritan, who was on a journey, came to where the man was. But when he saw him, he was moved with compassion. The Samaritan went to him and bandaged his wounds, tending them with oil and wine. Then he placed the wounded man on his own donkey, took him to an inn, and took care of him. The next day, he took two full days' worth of wages and gave them to the innkeeper. He said, 'Take care of him, and when I return, I will pay you back for any additional costs.'

What do you think? Which one of these three was a neighbor to the man who encountered thieves?"

Then the legal expert said, "The one who demonstrated mercy toward him."

Jesus told him, "Go and do likewise."

Luke 10:25-37

Reflect and Respond

As we see in this passage, we are commanded to love and serve the injured and forgotten, the helpless and the hopeless. When we think about our definition of community, and our commitment to love those in our inner circle, we must also acknowledge God's commands to love and serve those who are in need of our help. God calls all of us—the community of believers—to "defend the poor and fatherless; do justice to the afflicted and needy" (Psalm 82:3 NKJV), and God calls us to encourage and motivate one another to obey these commands.

When you read Luke 10:25-37, often referred to as the story of the Good Samaritan, what emotions does it stir in you? Do you feel compassion for the injured man, or anger at those who passed him by? Are you moved by the stranger's kindness and over-the-top mercy?

Read James 1:27. Why do you think this kind of devotion is considered "pure"?

When we think about the jumbled mess that is our world, and how much injustice there is, we can easily get overwhelmed and become paralyzed by the seemingly endless amount of work to be done. It's hard to know where to start! That is when we must remind each other that God is God and we are not. God knows every cry and every need, and we can be encouraged that we only have to be obedient to God's leading; God will direct us and guide our steps perfectly. We must simply be obedient to each step God leads us to take. We are free to be motivated, not by guilt or pride, but by the generous love and provision that God gives us. Since we have been given so much, and so freely, we are free to give generously to others.

When my husband and I first married, we were determined to share God's abundance with others. Despite the fact that we lived in a tiny house and were strapped financially, we opened our home to whomever—whether it was having people over for dinner (which was sometimes like the loaves and fishes story) or taking in the homeless (with only one bathroom!), we willingly put ourselves out there. And instead of feeling depleted or deprived for sharing what little we had, it seemed that God's blessings and abundance simply increased. More important, our lives were enriched.

Read Matthew 10:29-31. What do these verses tell you about God's watchful care?

Read Matthew 6:19-21. Consider how you use the resources that you have at your disposal. Whether little or much, are you using them to invest in the work of the Lord?

> We can easily get overwhelmed and become paralyzed by the seemingly endless amount of work to be done. . . . We only have to be obedient to God's leading; God will direct us and guide our steps perfectly.

119

When you think about the needs of those in your community, where are you encouraged to step up and take action? What needs pull at your heart and could benefit from your service?

In what specific ways can you encourage other believers to practice mercy— not out of guilt or pride, but out of the love and freedom we've been given in Christ?

Some of my favorite stories about mercy belong to my husband. And although I question that he occasionally picks up hitchhikers (and he forbids me to do this), I trust his discernment in this practice. Not long ago I received this e-mail from a store owner who'd met my husband and his unusual traveling companion [edited for brevity]:

My husband and I own and operate a small sporting goods store in [our town]. One quiet day, a couple of men came into our store. One was tall and clean-cut, while the other was short and dirty. To be quite honest, they just didn't go together. The tall man was your husband, and he had picked up the freezing, traveling fellow back in or around [your town]. I guess the hitchhiker was trying to make a warming fire by the roadside, when a police officer told him to put it out. Your husband then picked the man up and, eventually, came into my store to buy him something warm and dry for his feet. Well, we finally fit him in a pair of boots and some wool socks. After your husband paid, he went out to the car and got a copy of A Mother's Story, *signed by you, and gave it to me. I was so touched by this caring, sincere man. I remember that I wanted to give him a hug, but knew if I did, I would become a blubbering idiot!*

Well, after I read that sweet e-mail, I was the one who was the blubbering idiot, but sometimes I need to be reminded what a wonderful and merciful man I'm married to. No doubt you have your own stories. Recalling and sharing these stories helps to spur us on toward acts of mercy.

Talk to God

Lord, though there is pain and hardship and struggle, I believe you are working all things for good, even when we can't see it with our earthly eyes. Give me the strength and compassion to love others as you've loved me, and give me courage to step out of my comfort zone and serve those who need to be shown your love. Open my eyes to the needs around me, Lord. Amen.

As You Go

Has there been a ministry or a person to whom God has been drawing you to serve? Don't discount God's gentle (or maybe not-so-gentle) nudgings. How can you make steps today to get involved?

DAY 5: THE BEAUTY OF HERITAGE

Read God's Word

See what kind of love the Father has given to us in that we should be called God's children, and that is what we are!

1 John 3:1

Reflect and Respond

Each of us has a heritage. We are all products of many nations, many cultures, many personalities, many traditions, many communities. Some heritages are strong, passed down from generation to generation, lasting and enduring, while others are broken, the stories and traditions lost in the bustle of time and hardship and pain. No matter our heritage, we are shaped and molded by the communities in which we are raised.

Anna's Native American heritage is strong. Though her mother rejected it for many years, Anna embraced the ways of her Grandma Pearl's people. Coming back to the river strengthened Anna's connection to her grandmother and to her Siuslaw ancestors and helped Anna find the inner strength and resilience to begin a new life.

Anna's story was inspired in part by my husband, who is one-eighth Cherokee. One-eighth might not sound like much, but he was profoundly affected by that heritage nonetheless. His grandmother was half Cherokee, but because she'd been raised with cruel prejudice she tried to hide her ethnicity in her adulthood. Unfortunately this landed her in some dysfunctional and abusive relationships. As a result, her children suffered from many generational problems (including neglect, abuse, and abandonment). Ironically and despite these problems, there was also a lot of wisdom in the Native American side of this family. I'd see snippets of it in my mother-in-law's love and understanding of geology and plants and animals. Although she was a deeply troubled woman, she was

> Each of us has a heritage. . . . Some are strong . . . others are broken. . . . No matter our heritage, we are shaped and molded by the communities in which we are raised.

happy and fulfilled while experiencing God's creation. I always wanted to understand more about their Native American heritage and family history, but most of the older generation is gone now.

The word *heritage* has many synonyms—*legacy, inheritance, tradition, birthright.* All of these words point to the past, to something handed down to the next generation. Though Lauren originally rejected her Siuslaw heritage, she eventually realizes the legacy of strength that has been passed down through the women in her family. When Sarah disappears, Lauren claims that same strength for her daughter and prays it will carry her home.

Excerpt from *River's Call,* Chapter 30

"Sarah is going to be just fine, Mom. I know it." Lauren made a shaky smile. *"Remember what you used to tell me. Sarah has to paddle her own canoe."* She shook her head. *"And I'm sure she can do a better job of paddling a canoe than me. Unlike her inept mother, Sarah probably won't tip her canoe over in the middle of the river."*

"You're right," Anna agreed. *"Sarah is adept in a canoe."*

"I'll bet that she shows up here," Lauren assured her. *"Probably by the end of the week."*

"I hope you're right." Anna reached for Lauren's hand and turned them to face the river. *"Just the same, let's pray for her. Let's ask God to watch over her, to protect her, to guide her back home."* And that was what they did, there on the banks of the Siuslaw, they prayed that Sarah Pearl would safely find her way home. *"Really, that's all we can do right now,"* Anna admitted after they said "amen." Then, as they continued to walk, Anna was reminded of her ancestors. Certainly they'd been through some very hard times, and yet here she was—she and Lauren—descendants of a very troubled people.

"You know that your great-great-grandmother lived on the banks of the Siuslaw," Anna told Lauren as they walked through the wooded area. *"Her name was Little Flower, but it was later changed to Anna."*

"Like you." Lauren bent down to pick a buttercup, handing it to her mother.

"Yes." Anna smelled the tiny bloom. *"Little Flower lost both her parents to smallpox when she was only three years old."*

"Who took care of her?"

"Relatives."

"The smallpox epidemic was brought here by the moving man."

"That's the white man, right?"

"That's right. Little Flower's life was relatively calm for a few years, but when she was about Sarah's age, she and her people were forced off their land and sent to the reservation." Anna told about how the Siuslaw were herded like animals, forced to walk for days and days on the beach, and finally placed on the reservation up north. *"The*

ones who survived were placed there for reeducation," Anna explained. "That meant they were supposed to go from being Indian to being white. The women and girls were taught to cook and sew like white women and to speak English. The men mostly died." Now she told about how her great-grandfather was shot for trying to find food. "Although many of them were starving, they were not allowed to hunt or fish or gather their native foods."

Lauren turned to Anna. "I never knew this . . . not any of it."

"Then it's time you knew." Anna continued to tell her of the hardships of their ancestors and how, finally, the few surviving Native Americans were given parcels of land. "It was a small token compared to the land they used to occupy. And it was only made available to those who knew how to file a land claim. Thankfully, my great-grandmother and her sister figured it out." Anna smiled. "We come from a long line of smart women."

Lauren chuckled. "Wish I'd known that sooner."

"My grandmother, Grandma Pearl, inherited this land from her mother. Grandma Pearl and her first husband built the first cabin, the one that Hazel stays in now."

"Yes." Lauren nodded. "Hazel has told me a little about Grandma Pearl. She sounds like she was an interesting woman."

Anna told Lauren about how Grandma Pearl returned to the old ways, how she befriended other Siuslaw women and how they tried to relearn the way their ancestors had lived. "But it was hard. So much was lost, so many stories forgotten. But Grandma Pearl did her best to preserve it." She put a hand on Lauren's shoulder. "Do you know why I'm telling you this now?"

"I'm not sure. But I like hearing about it."

The trail was coming alongside the river now. "The Siuslaw were a matriarchal society, Lauren. That means that the inheritance is passed down through the women. And someday, Shining Waters will belong to you."

Lauren's brow creased. "I hope that's not for a long, long time, Mom. I wouldn't be ready for it now."

"It will happen at the right time, Lauren. And then, one day, you will hand it on to Sarah." They stopped walking now, turning to look at the river which was sparkling like diamonds in the bright sunshine.

"What an amazing heritage."

Anna nodded. "It's a heritage of mercy and second chances, Lauren. From our ancestors to me, from me to you, from you to Sarah . . . for eternity." With misty eyes, Anna gazed out over the shining waters as she prayed for her granddaughter's canoe to remain sure and safe and sound . . . and to turn around toward home.

• • • • • • •

In a few words or phrases, how would you describe your own heritage?

What aspects of your heritage—the things handed down to you from your family—do you embrace?

Are there aspects of your heritage that you have rejected? If so, why?

No matter our heritages . . . we are loved and provided for by a God who will never fail us.

Because our heritages are given to us through fallible human beings, sins and flaws are also often passed down from generation to generation. In fact, because of this many of us reject our heritages entirely, vowing that we will be different, that we will pass down a new heritage to our children and grandchildren. No matter our heritages, how wonderful it is to know that we are loved and provided for by a God who will never fail us. We've considered 1 John 3:1 in previous weeks, but it's a verse we should consider again and again on our journey to healing: "See what kind of love the Father has given to us in that we should be called God's children, and that is what we are!" We are the children of God, and that heritage is strong and perfect.

What do the following verses have to say about the heritage we have in Christ?

Psalm 68:5

Matthew 6:25-34

Matthew 7:9-11

How are you encouraged to know that, above all, you are God's child, and God has passed down to you a heritage that is perfect—one that you can confidently claim as your own?

Talk to God

Abba Father, I know that you have presided over every aspect of my story, including the family I was born into and the heritage that was waiting for me there. But Lord, I thank you that you have redeemed me and called me your own, and that I am not bound by that earthly heritage; rather, I have been given a new name and a new story in you. Amen.

As You Go

Spend some time today in prayer, meditating on 1 John 3:1. Pray for the clarity and courage to claim God's promises as a child of God. Journal your thoughts as you have time (journaling pages are provided at the back of the book).

You are God's child, and God has passed down to you a heritage that is perfect— one that you can confidently claim as your own.

125

VIDEO NOTES
A FEW MINUTES WITH MELODY

INTERESTING INSIGHTS:

POINTS I'D LIKE TO DISCUSS WITH THE GROUP:

THEME 3

Healing Brings
New Beginnings

River's End

BEFORE YOU BEGIN

Book Summary: *River's End*

It is 1978, and it has been two years since Sarah, Anna's granddaughter, disappeared from the inn. With no word from Sarah, Anna fears the worst but continues to hope that Sarah will one day return. On Sarah's eighteenth birthday, she shows up at the inn, thin and ragged, having lived in a commune for the last two years. Sarah is bitter and confused, harboring deep anger against her parents over her neglected childhood. Sarah doesn't want to see her mother, Lauren, so Anna suggests Lauren take a vacation from her job at the inn so that Sarah will stay and recuperate.

Soon Clark's mother, Hazel, returns to the inn to settle in after her retirement and a trip to the Far East, and her presence seems to encourage Sarah's healing even more. When Lauren comes back to the inn, she and Sarah steer clear of one another, as Sarah is not yet ready to reconcile with her mother.

Meanwhile, as Anna dreams up new visions for the inn, Clark takes her on a surprise picnic to a breathtaking piece of land he has secretly bought for her. Clark hopes that the land, which overlooks the point where the river ends and the ocean begins, will be the perfect spot to build a getaway house for the two of them. Anna is touched but overwhelmed by Clark's plans due to all the work to be done at the inn, and so Clark agrees to abandon the idea.

When Hazel has an episode with her heart and is admitted to the hospital, Sarah chooses to leave the river once again, fearing that her bitterness is affecting everyone at the inn. In a goodbye note to Anna, Sarah reveals that she is filled with shame over her past actions and feels worthless. Anna pursues Sarah to her old commune, but discovers that Sarah has already left. Desperate to not give up on Sarah, Anna vows to continue her search.

Ready for a new start, Lauren decides to go back to college and to pursue the degree she never finished. Although her health is declining rapidly, an ailing Hazel continues to encourage and mentor Lauren and the other women at the inn. In early October Hazel dies, leaving everyone grieving but celebrating her life. During this time, Lauren vows to continue the search for Sarah and never give up on her. When Lauren finds an ailing Sarah at a commune in California, Anna and Clark help bring her home.

Ill and ashamed, Sarah agrees to return to the inn to recover, moving into Hazel's cabin. As she begins to feel better and regain some hope, Sarah considers going back to school and following in Hazel's footsteps by studying anthropology and sociology. Sarah goes on to earn her high school diploma and is accepted into the university.

In the fall, while Sarah is getting ready to leave for school, Donald shows up, apologizing for the past mistakes he'd made as her father. Sarah, whose heart is beginning to heal, accepts his apology and forgives her father.

Lauren, still living away from the river for Sarah's sake, begins to hope for new life for herself as well when she meets Brad, a sculptor with Native American heritage. Soon they are engaged, with plans to marry at the inn over the holidays. Though Anna is thrilled about all the good things happening in the lives of those she loves, she is left spinning by all the changes happening around her.

As Christmas approaches and Lauren's wedding nears, Anna fears that her daughter and granddaughter may never reconcile. She encourages Sarah to let go of her bitterness for her own health and well-being, and to forgive her mother. Sarah seems reluctant but, on Christmas morning, Sarah releases years of anger and frustration and forgives her mother. Lauren and Brad marry in a ceremony at the river, with Sarah as her maid of honor.

Filled with hope and happiness, Anna believes nothing could be more perfect and is shocked and surprised when Clark takes her to the river's end property and reveals a house he has secretly been building for her. The amazing home is more than Anna could have dreamed of, a wonderful place to spend their retirement years.

River's End concludes in the summer 2010 as Anna and her family gather at the Inn at Shining Waters to celebrate fifty years of the inn's operation. Surrounded by many generations of her family—including Sarah and Sarah's children and grandchildren—Anna is overcome by the amazing heritage and legacy of Shining Waters. It has become everything she ever dreamed it would be—a place of resilience and family, of healing and restoration.

Character Sketches

Sarah

Sarah (Anna's granddaughter) is like a mini-Anna, except that she's growing up in a less nurturing environment. But thanks to Anna's influence during her early years, Sarah seems to be on track. She is, by nature, sensitive, thoughtful, intuitive, helpful, gracious, and fairly mature for her age. But after years of being practically ignored by her selfish mother, Sarah enters into her own rebellion during adolescence. In her mind, she is grown up enough to be on her own. Hasn't she been taking care of herself for years? So she runs away with a boyfriend only to find herself living in communes. She's seeking spiritual truth and life answers but in all the wrong places. When she returns to the river, she still has questions and struggles. She is on her spiritual journey, but her inability to forgive her mother (Lauren) cripples her. Until she forgives Lauren, she is unable to heal and move forward.

Brad

Brad's mom is Native American and his dad is Caucasian. Although he was raised in white culture, he enjoyed the times he and his mom visited the reservation where his relatives lived. However, he never completely fit in there—or anywhere. As an adult he went to live on the "rez" and started drinking. Many years and struggles later, he recovered from alcoholism and turned to art. As a talented bronze sculptor, he now expresses himself through beautiful works of art that reflect nature. Ironically, he meets Lauren, who wouldn't have given him the time of day when she was young, and they hit it off. Brad is very drawn to Anna's world on the river. He feels like he has come home.

Jewel

Jewel's had a hard life. Her dad took off when she was ten, and her mom had a string of boyfriends. Neglected and abused, Jewel got involved in drugs in her early teens and ran away from home a few years later. Like Sarah, she's been looking for an ideal home and community. She longs for structure and love and stability. Unfortunately, she has either looked in the wrong places or been tricked. But when she gets the opportunity to be "adopted" into Anna's tribe, she grabs onto it. For a while she probably fills Anna's void for Sarah, who is still running and struggling.

WEEK 6
THE POWER OF TRANSFORMATION

Scripture for the Week

*The L*ORD *works righteousness;*
does justice for all who are oppressed....
*The L*ORD *has established his throne in heaven,*
and his kingdom rules over all.
Psalm 103:6, 19

Excerpt from *River's End,* Chapter 3

"*S*arah, I'm just so glad you're [home]." Anna smiled at her. "I have missed you so much these past two years. You have absolutely no idea. It was like a piece of me was gone. Can you understand that?"

Sarah seemed to soften now. "I missed you too, Grandma."

"And I have to admit that it still hurts to think you never tried to contact me...just to say you were alive," Anna confessed, "but I do understand. I know we sometimes do things that seem justified at the time...things we might look back on later, wondering if we could've done it differently." Now Anna told Sarah a bit about how it was for her when Lauren was a small child...how she might've done it differently.

"But I was so overwhelmed with caring for Lauren's father. His physical injuries from the war were serious enough and he was certainly in pain, but the wounds in his mind were the hardest part. I felt I needed to protect Lauren from his outbursts and mood swings. It seemed too much for a child to witness. For that reason, Lauren was left in the care of her grandmother Eunice...far more than I would have liked. However, at the time, I didn't see any other solution."

"I'm sure you did the best you could."

Anna shrugged. "After Adam died, I stayed on with Eunice. I know it was partly because I was so worn down by the years of caring for him, almost as if I'd lost a part of myself. I just didn't know what to do, how to start my life over again. And by then Eunice was such an enormous part of Lauren's life, and she'd just lost her father, it seemed cruel to take that away from Lauren as well. But, as you know, Eunice spoiled Lauren. She gave into her about everything." She sighed. "And I suppose I allowed it. Oh, I'd try to stand up to her, but it was like standing up to a tidal wave. I really should've left much sooner. But I didn't. So, to be fair, you should partially blame me for how Lauren was so immature and ill prepared for adulthood when she became your mother. It was like a child raising a child."

Sarah's brow creased as if she was trying to take this in.

"Sometimes I've thought that if I'd just had the strength to take Lauren away from there, and if I'd brought her here to the river, back when she was still a child, I think about how everything would've turned out so differently." She sighed. "You see how it's easy to blame myself and feel guilty over this. But that's when I try to remember that I did the best I could at the time. What's done is done and I simply have to trust God with the rest of it."

"I really don't see how you could blame yourself for Lauren's mistakes."

"Yes . . . but maybe it comes with being a mother. You always want the best for your children and your grandchildren." Now she smiled. "But then I have to remember that if I'd brought Lauren out here as a child, she never would've met and married Donald and then you wouldn't have been born. And that would've been very sad for me. In the long run, I do think that things do turn out for the best."

"I wish I believed that was true." Sarah pulled the afghan up over her shoulders, shivering as if she were cold.

"Maybe you will in time. We all do things we regret," Anna said quietly, "when we are young and foolish. When we're older, we realize that we have to forgive. It's as constant as the river."

> "We all do things we regret," Anna said quietly, "when we are young and foolish. When we're older, we realize that we have to forgive. It's as constant as the river."

· · · · · · ·

DAY 1: GOD OF SECOND CHANCES

Read God's Word

By faith Abraham, when called to go to a place he would later receive as his inheritance, obeyed and went, even though he did not know where he was going. By faith he made his home in the promised land like a stranger in a foreign country; he lived in tents, as did Isaac and Jacob, who were heirs with him of the same promise. For he was looking forward to the city with foundations, whose architect and builder is God. And by faith even Sarah, who was past childbearing age, was enabled to bear children because she considered him faithful who had made the promise. And so from this one man, and he as good as dead, came descendants as numerous as the stars in the sky and as countless as the sand on the seashore.

Hebrews 11:8-12

Reflect and Respond

Hebrews chapter 11 is often referred to as "the faith chapter," a book of the Bible dedicated to men and women who had great faith and through whom God did great things. These men and women are considered heroes of our faith, their lives great pictures of how God uses people to accomplish His purposes. But although we celebrate their faith, their stories are not without bumps and detours along the way.

Take Abraham, whom you just read about. Even though God promised Abraham and his wife, Sarah, that they would conceive and have a child in spite of their old age, they couldn't believe that would actually happen. They took matters into their own hands and made a huge mess of things. But God had plans for this couple and didn't give up on them. God kept his promise that Sarah would give birth to a child and made good on His promise to make Abraham the father of many nations.

And consider Moses. Born a Jew but raised in the house of Egypt's pharaoh, Moses killed a man in anger and fled to the desert. Knowing he couldn't go home again, Moses resigned himself to a life of desert living, marrying and settling down as a shepherd. But God pursued Moses and called him into service, choosing him to be the instrument by which all the Jews in Egypt would be saved.

Our God is one who pursues us, even when we are reluctant. That pursuit is the theme of the story of Jonah, an unlikely prophet:

> The LORD's word came to Jonah, Amittai's son: "Get up and go to Nineveh, that great city, and cry out against it, for their evil has come to my attention." So Jonah got up—to flee to Tarshish from the LORD! He went down to Jaffa and found a ship headed for Tarshish. He paid the fare and went aboard to go with them to Tarshish, away from the LORD.
>
> Jonah 1:1-3

Jonah, afraid of the violent, irreverent, and downright scary Ninevites, booked the first ship out of town. He literally ran away to avoid the Lord's call on his life. His plan was to escape God, but God wasn't ready to let Jonah go.

Read Jonah chapters 1 and 2. What strikes you most about Jonah's story? In what ways do you identify with Jonah?

Our God is one who pursues us, even when we are reluctant.

Jonah 1:1 says, "The LORD's word came to Jonah." Have you ever received a word from the Lord—a message you knew was directed to you personally? What happened? How did you respond?

After his encounter with the fish, "the LORD's word came to Jonah a second time" (3:1). Once again, God commanded Jonah, and this time, doubly assured of God's call on his life, Jonah obeyed. Though Jonah's story continued down a somewhat rocky road, God accomplished His purposes through Jonah, and the people of Ninevah believed in Jonah's God.

God uses broken people to show the world His indestructible love.

Have you ever witnessed God working through someone who seemed like an unlikely source? What happened?

Has there ever been a time when you felt that God worked through you to reach someone, even though you felt unworthy or incapable?

God uses broken people to show the world His indestructible love. Abraham doubted. Sarah laughed. Moses and Jonah both ran. But God wasn't finished with any of them, and God's not finished with you either.

God doesn't keep a tally of our mistakes and shortcomings. We tend to limit God by expecting that He will react like us—that He will get angry and hold grudges and be deeply disappointed when we fail. But, over and over again, Scripture tells us that is not who God is, and it's not who Jesus is either.

God was so willing to claim you as his own that He sent Jesus to earth to make that happen: "God so loved the world that he gave his only Son, so that everyone who believes in him won't perish but will have eternal life. God didn't send his Son into the world to judge the world, but that the world might be saved through him" (John 3:16-17).

What do you think of the idea that the Lord is actively pursuing you? What emotions does that idea stir in you?

Just as Anna and Lauren refused to give up on their search for Sarah, so God pursues you with a desire to restore and protect you. How are you responding to God's pursuit? Are you running away in fear? Do you doubt that God is even looking for you? Do you feel as if you have it all under control—that you don't need to be pursued and rescued? Where is your heart today?

Talk to God

God, you never give up on me, and I praise you for that. Make me willing to be found, Lord, willing to run into your arms and rest in your perfect love. Thank you for never giving up on me, for not keeping a score of my mistakes but delighting in giving me your pure righteousness. Amen.

As You Go

Today, prayerfully consider how you are responding to God's relentless pursuit for your heart. Do you doubt, like Abraham? Laugh, like Sarah? Do you run, like Moses and Jonah? Confess your actions to God and thank Him for His unfailing goodness and love.

DAY 2: CHRIST'S TRANSFORMING POWER

Read God's Word

The LORD works righteousness;
does justice for all who are oppressed.
Psalm 103:6

Reflect and Respond

People use many words when they talk about the Christian faith—*justice, righteousness, justification*. But what do these words mean?

We've already discovered that God is about second chances—that God relentlessly pursues our hearts. Even after we come to faith in God and believe in the redeeming or saving work of Jesus on the cross, God continues to pursue and transform us. Psalm 103:6 says, "The LORD works righteousness." To be righteous means to obey God's law and all its demands—basically, an impossible task for humankind. God is not just devoted to justice; God is justice. Justice is a part of God's nature, God's perfection; and it is something God demands for His creation.

The people of the Old Testament were consumed by their efforts to keep the law so that they might remain in right standing with God. Though God gave them rules to live by for their own safety and protection, there was no way that they could keep all of them. It was inevitable that they were going to mess up; there was just too much to remember, and sin was too much part of their nature. So, they would offer a sacrifice to God as payment for their sin and disobedience in order to be forgiven and remain in right relationship with God.

> We should not be tricked or deceived into thinking we have to do better or try harder to gain God's favor. God has claimed us as His own, and He will never let us go.

From the beginning of time, God had a plan to purify and redeem all of creation—to free us from sin and the penalty of sin. God sent His son, Jesus, to be a sinless man and take on the weight of the sins of the world by becoming the perfect, ultimate sacrifice. He was the fulfillment of the law and the bridge from us to God the Father. (See 2 Corinthians 5:17 and Romans 4:6-8.) Through Jesus, the LORD "worked our righteousness"—our justification, our fulfillment of the law—so that we could have communion and an intimate relationship with Him.

What does it mean to you that you have been redeemed (set free from sin) and justified (made right with God)?

How has Jesus' sacrifice transformed your life?

Psalm 103:6 says that God "does justice for all who are oppressed." Who are the oppressed? We are. We were oppressed by our own sinful nature, and so God did justice for us. Because we were incapable of doing it ourselves, God sent Jesus to fulfill the law for us.

God declared us right with the law and bestowed His freedom and love upon us. He transformed us into those who are perfect through faith in Jesus Christ and are entitled to the benefits and advantages of being perfected creatures. God is the Great Transformer, the one who redeems our lives.

When we are feeling stuck, defeated by our own sin and shortcomings, we can turn our eyes to God and remember that He is the one who transforms our lives. God is working in us day by day, minute by minute, to help us get past ourselves so that we may be able to see Him more clearly.

Do you ever feel oppressed by sin—either yours or someone else's? Explain.

Even though we are discouraged and held back by our sin, the beautiful thing about justification is that sin can't claim us anymore. We no longer belong to our sinful selves—the old has gone, the new has come (see 2 Corinthians 5:17). We should not be tricked or deceived into thinking we have to do better or try harder to gain God's favor. God has claimed us as His own, and He will never let us go.

God has claimed us as His own, but that doesn't mean we won't sometimes feel the effects of a fallen world. When Adam went to war and returned home broken, the aftermath of a horrible war reverberated in his life and in the lives of many others. In his death Anna lost her husband and lost herself in guilt; Eunice lost her only son and consigned herself to a life of bitterness; Lauren lost her father and watched her mother fade away.

How have you felt the effects of our fallen world?

Read Romans 7:14-15, 25. How do you identify with the words of the Apostle Paul?

When we are weak and discouraged, God is there for us, offering hope and healing to our weary hearts. Read Romans 5:1-5. How does this passage speak to you today?

What does it mean to you that "hope does not disappoint" (v. 5)?

Talk to God

God, I am amazed at what you've done for me—how you've lifted me out of my own sin and helplessness and given me a new name and a new heart. You have transformed my life, and for that I give you praise. Hallelujah! What a savior. Amen.

As You Go

Colossians 2:6-8 says, "So live in Christ Jesus the LORD in the same way as you received him. Be rooted and built up in him, be established in faith, and overflow with thanksgiving just as you were taught." How is God encouraging you to live in Him today?

> Though we want to claim God's promises for our lives and hold tightly to them, the noise of our lives often takes over, and we can easily get lost and forget how loved we are.

DAY 3: DAILY MERCY

Read God's Word

So we aren't depressed. But even if our bodies are breaking down on the outside, the person that we are on the inside is being renewed every day.

2 Corinthians 4:16

Reflect and Respond

Not only are God's mercies perfect and complete, they are abundant—an endless, daily source of strength and encouragement for our weary hearts.

As women, we need daily renewing! Each day the demands made on our lives can seem endless and draining: Your job requires more of your nights and weekends than you anticipated. The piled-up laundry and dishes taunt you as you rush by them, struggling to get the kids fed and to school on time. A friend calls and needs to talk in the midst of a hectic day of errands. You and your husband finally plan a date night out, but the sitter cancels at the last minute.

Some days it seems that we can hardly take a breath, that we will never catch up to all the things on our to-do lists, that we'll never be able to see past our front doors. When we are emotionally and physically tapped out, our spiritual lives tend to suffer as well. Though we want to claim God's promises for our lives and hold tightly to them, the noise of our lives often takes over, and we can easily get lost and forget how loved we are.

In *River's End,* we see Sarah, blinded by pain and desperate for healing and security, suffering physically. Frustrated by her search for peace and for happiness, Sarah's inner torture begins to severely affect her health, and she is in a bad state when Lauren finally finds her in the sick room of a commune. Today's Scripture verse, 2 Corinthians 4:16, encourages us that even though our bodies are physically breaking down, God is renewing who we are on the inside each and every day! Here is even more encouragement from the prophet Isaiah:

Don't you know? Haven't you heard? The LORD *is the everlasting God, the creator of the ends of the earth. He doesn't grow tired or weary. His understanding is beyond human reach, giving power to the tired and reviving the exhausted. Youths will become tired and weary, young men will certainly stumble; but those who hope in the* LORD *will renew their strength; they will fly up on wings like eagles; they will run and not be tired; they will walk and not be weary.*

Isaiah 40:28-31

What encouragement do these two Scripture passages give you?

God wants to renew us—to continually give us His love and strength. So, what can we do to hear God's voice above the noise in our lives? How can we quiet our world and learn to hear this voice that seeks to renew and transform us?

I'm blessed to live in a beautiful place and, like Anna in my novels, I feel closer to God in the midst of creation. When I need to quiet my heart and experience God more intimately, I usually take a walk in the woods or by the ocean. But I can also experience God by closing my eyes and taking a few deep breaths . . . and just waiting. God is always here with us; we just need to make the choice to stop and listen.

Read the following verses. What does each say about training our minds to better hear God's voice?

Romans 12:2

Philippians 4:8

Colossians 3:2

1 Peter. 1:13

As you go about your day, do you intentionally stop to hear the Lord's voice speaking to you, or do you find it hard to make the time and space for that?

How can you begin the practice of renewing your mind daily with the words of the Lord? Maybe you can't commit to sitting down for an hour to focus on the Bible. That's okay. You can spend time in prayer in the shower or in the carpool line. You can tape an encouraging verse to your mirror so that you can read it as you brush your teeth. What can you do to reclaim some time in your day and devote it to pursuing God's voice?

Talk to God

Jesus, speak your words of life to me today. Open my ears to hear your sweet voice, words that affirm me with life and healing. Transform my mind and my heart so that in all things I desire you above all else. Give me strength, patience, and joy to face the day ahead. Amen.

As You Go

Meditate on these words of the old hymn "Jesus, Still Lead On":

> When we seek relief
> From a long-felt grief
> When temptations come alluring,
> Make us patient and enduring;
> Show us that bright shore
> Where we weep no more.
>
> Jesus, still lead on.
> (Nicolaus L. von Zinzendorf)

Ask God to speak words of life to you today, and to enable you to hear them clearly.

DAY 4: THE TRANSFORMING POWER OF PRAYER

Read God's Word

Then you shall call, and the LORD will answer; You shall cry, and He will say, "Here I am."

Isaiah 58:9

Reflect and Respond

When life seems too hard, when the challenges feel too consuming, when we come to the end of our resources and capacity, we can trust that God is there and is listening to us. The act of prayer—of simply talking to God and asking for help and wisdom—is powerful. Prayer is not a spiritual exercise that will make us more holy or more pleasing to God. Instead, it is an intimate conversation with one who loves us deeply and longs to be in relationship with us.

We pray, not in order to make ourselves feel better or to demand that God do what we want, but because prayer is a direct line of communication with Almighty God. It is a gift that we have received through Jesus' death on the cross, and it is a gift we can confidently claim. Hebrews 4:16 says, "Let us therefore come boldly to the throne of grace, that we may obtain mercy and find grace to help in time of need" (NKJV).

> When life seems too hard . . . we can trust that God is there and is listening to us. The act of prayer . . . is powerful.

What is your view on prayer? Do you view it as a spiritual discipline? As a privilege? As a necessity? As a tool of change?

Consider what Scripture has to say about the importance and purpose of prayer. What does each of these verses say about prayer?

Ephesians 6:18

1 Thessalonians 5:17

Romans 8:26

James 5:16

Do you believe God answers prayer? Explain.

Do you truly believe prayer has the power to change your life, and the lives of others? Why or why not?

"Let us therefore come boldly to the throne of grace, that we may obtain mercy and find grace to help in time of need." (Hebrews 4:16 NKJV)

Read 1 Thessalonians 5:27. What do you think it means to "pray without ceasing"?

Throughout the Bible, we see the importance of intercession—of praying on behalf of and for others.

Read Jesus' prayer for us in John 17:9-24. What part of this prayer stands out to you?

Jesus' prayer life shows us how to pray for one another. We are to pray that God would rescue and save and turn the hearts of His children toward home.

Excerpt from *River's End*, Chapter 11

Anna felt a smidgeon of hope as she turned back up the river. Sarah and the missing boat had to be on the river somewhere.

But [Anna] wasn't completely sure of this. It was something she was trying not to consider, but Anna and Clark both knew if the boat wasn't on the river—there was another place it might possibly be—the ocean. Everyone knew that if you continued on past Florence, beyond the bridge and through the jetties, there was only one place left to go. And that little river skiff wouldn't last long out there.

But as she headed on upriver, she didn't want to think about that possibility. Not yet, anyway. Instead, she prayed. With all her heart and soul, she prayed. And as she prayed she got a very strange sensation that others were praying with her. As odd as it seemed, it felt as if all the other river people, the ones who had passed, were agreeing with her prayer. She could feel her grandmother and her mother and father and even Babette . . . so strongly . . . as if they were all praying for Sarah's safety too.

• • • • • • •

Anna loves her daughter and granddaughter deeply, though she is often baffled by their life choices. When she feels helpless and afraid and worried for her family, Anna finds that the best thing she can do for them is pray.

Have any of your relationships left you feeling helpless and at a loss about what to do? How so?

Have you prayed for those people and situations? Have you seen God move yet? If so, how?

How can praying for others and asking God to "bring them home" change our relationships with those we love?

How might prayer bring freedom and healing into any of your relationships?

We are to pray that God would rescue and save and turn the hearts of His children toward home.

Talk to God

Lord, though I cannot see you or audibly hear your voice, I believe that you speak to me and that you listen to me when I pray. I claim the promises in Scripture that assure me that you hear me and that you want a relationship with me. As I pray, turn my heart away from my own shortcomings and limitations and point me toward you. Thank you for hearing my prayers for those I love. Remind me of the power of praying for others in your name. Amen.

As You Go

Read the story in Acts 16:25-34 about what happened as Paul and Silas prayed in prison. As they prayed, an earthquake shook the jail and the doors of their cells flew open. But God was after more than their freedom; God was after the hearts of the jailer and his family, who came to trust in God that night. What do you imagine Paul and Silas might have prayed that night? How did their prayers bring about transformation?

DAY 5: NEW LIFE FOR OUR RELATIONSHIPS

Read God's Word

They approached Joseph and said, "Your father gave orders before he died, telling us, 'This is what you should say to Joseph. "Please, forgive your brothers' sins and misdeeds, for they did terrible things to you. Now, please forgive the sins of the servants of your father's God."'" Joseph wept when they spoke to him. His brothers wept too, fell down in front of him, and said, "We're here as your slaves." But Joseph said to them, "Don't be afraid. Am I God? You planned something bad for me, but God produced something good from it, in order to save the lives of many people, just as he's doing today."

Genesis 50:16-20

Reflect and Respond

Today's Scripture tells the end of the story of Joseph and his brothers—a story about relationships, pain, regret, and ultimately forgiveness and new life. Likewise, The Inn at Shining Water Series is filled with similar themes. Many of the characters harbor regret in their relationships. Anna regrets setting a bad example for Lauren and not standing up to Eunice during Lauren's childhood. Eunice regrets living in many years of bitterness toward Anna. Lauren regrets not being there for Sarah as she grew up. Sarah regrets running away and hurting her grandmother. But from a place of regret, grace can be found, as Sarah ultimately finds in her relationship with Anna. After years of running from her family, Sarah finally comes home to stay and begins to deal with her pain.

Excerpt from *River's End,* Chapter 22

"I've been so awful, Grandma." Sarah stepped back now, looking directly at Anna. "I've hurt you and Grandpa so much. I don't deserve you being kind to me. Why are you being so good to me? Especially after I've been so bad?"

"Because you're my granddaughter and I love you." Now Anna couldn't hold back her own tears. It seemed she'd been holding them back for days . . . maybe weeks . . . and months. She hugged Sarah again. "I'm so glad you're home, Sarah. So very glad." Now she held her at arm's length and just smiled at her. "I missed you so much."

"Grandma," Sarah said solemnly. "You know you saved my life. I honestly don't think I'd be alive if you hadn't come for me . . . brought me home."

Anna pulled a handkerchief from her sweater pocket; using it to wipe her eyes she then handed it to Sarah. "Not just me, sweetheart. We all worked together to help you. Your grandpa, Jewel, Dr. Albers . . . even your mom."

"But it was really you," Sarah said with conviction. "You were behind it all, Grandma. I wouldn't be here without you."

"You are part of me, Sarah. And I felt like something in me was broken when you were missing. It was as if a part of me was gone."

"I'm sorry." Sarah sniffed. "I know I hurt you, Grandma. And, really, I'm sorry. Really, really sorry. I wish I could go back and do it differently."

Anna smoothed Sarah's hair back away from her face and smiled. "There's no going back . . . only forward. I'm just glad you're home—and that you're getting well. And I hope you realize that this is your home. You will always have a home here on the river. And we will always love you, Sarah, no matter what you do or where you go. You will always be part of us and we'll be a part of you."

From a place of regret, grace can be found.

• • • • • • •

Many of us live with regret over our pasts, and the regret only runs deeper when we realize our choices and actions have affected those we love. Each of our journeys is not without pain and hardship, but we can know that there is hope for the journey.

Let's take a closer look at Joseph's story in the book of Genesis. Joseph was Jacob's youngest and most favorite son. When his jealous brothers couldn't take him anymore, they sold him into slavery in Egypt. From there Joseph's journey took many twists and turns until eventually, many years later, he became the second most powerful man in Egypt. When a famine drove his brothers to Egypt for help, Joseph recognized them and ultimately forgave them for what they had put him through. His family was reunited, and his father regained a son.

Years later, after their father died, his brothers came to Joseph, afraid he might retaliate against them for their past actions. This is where today's Scripture reading takes up the story. The brothers asked Joseph to forgive their sins, acknowledging that they had done terrible things to him. Joseph and his brothers wept, and the brothers even offered to be his slaves. If Joseph had held a grudge, he could have taken this opportunity to punish his brothers in revenge. Instead he told them not to be afraid and humbly acknowledged that God had always been in control, working his situation for the good of many.

Joseph's story is a reminder that God is in control of each of our stories. God is the sovereign Lord, who brings good through all circumstances for those who love Him (1 Corinthians 2:9). No matter your story or the events of your life, God is watching over you. The things others have done that have affected you—whether intentionally or unintentionally—will be redeemed through God's perfect plan for your life.

The things others have done that have affected you—whether intentionally or unintentionally—will be redeemed through God's perfect plan for your life.

Does Joseph's story encourage you? If so, how?

How do you think you would have reacted in his situation? What would have been most difficult for you?

How have you been wounded in your life? How might God be redeeming and transforming that hurt?

Have you hurt others in the past? How might God redeem and transform that hurt?

I remember the years that I regretted my upbringing. Because my father was an abusive alcoholic, my parents' marriage ended when I was a toddler. Growing up in a single-parent home in the sixties, when it seemed everyone else was as "happy and normal" as some of the family sitcoms I enjoyed, I felt like I'd missed the boat. As a young adult I continued to feel deprived, but with years and experience I began to discover that many of those "happy" families had problems of their own. I also began to be more appreciative of my wonderful extended family of loving aunts and grandparents. Finally, I came to realize that many of my earlier challenges are the very things that make me the writer I am today—particularly for teen readers. My less-than-perfect life allows me to relate better to theirs.

Some amount of regret is inevitable in each of our lives, but we must be careful that it doesn't consume and paralyze us. Instead, we should turn our hurt, regret, and wounded relationships over to God, asking God to forgive and to heal and to lead us back to restoration in our relationships, for God is the only one who can truly heal and restore. Psalm 103:19 proclaims, "The LORD has established his throne in heaven, and his kingdom rules over all."

God has the power and authority to redeem our bad choices and circumstances, and God hears us when we call out to Him. In Matthew 7:7-8 Jesus says, "Ask, and you will receive. Search, and you will find. Knock, and the door will be opened to you. For everyone who asks, receives. Whoever seeks, finds. And to everyone who knocks, the door is opened." Since we know that God desires restoration and healing, we can confidently come to Him, asking for our broken and battered relationships to be transformed.

How does it make you feel to realize that God is the only one with the power to transform your relationships? And how does that knowledge change your perspective on reconciliation?

Often we need to allow others time and space to heal from our actions–time for God to prepare their hearts for reconciliation.

In *River's End*, Lauren is desperate to make amends with Sarah, but she knows that Sarah needs time to heal and to prepare for Lauren's apologies. Often we need to allow others time and space to heal from our actions—time for God to prepare their hearts for reconciliation. Trust God to work in the hearts of those with whom you desire to reconcile, and then act in obedience when God calls you to make amends. As author and pastor Max Lucado writes, "Go to the effort. Invest the time. Write the letter. Make the apology. Take the trip. Purchase the gift. Do it. The seized opportunity renders joy. The neglected brings regret."[2]

What action is God leading you to take toward someone in your life today?

Talk to God

Lord God, I praise you for your unending goodness and vision. You know how I long to control and manipulate every aspect of my life and my relationships, but I know that my efforts alone fall short. I pray for the strength and courage to trust you, and for your wisdom to guide my life. Lead me, Lord. Transform my life and my relationships with others. I praise you for your love. Amen.

As You Go

In God's time, He *will* transform and renew. Our God of second chances—of many chances— redeems. Today, is God calling you to wait on Him to redeem and restore, or is He nudging you to act toward reconciliation? Journal your thoughts (journaling pages are provided at the back of the book).

VIDEO NOTES
A FEW MINUTES WITH MELODY

INTERESTING INSIGHTS:

POINTS I'D LIKE TO DISCUSS WITH THE GROUP:

WEEK 7
BEAUTY IN NEW BEGINNINGS

Scripture for the Week

But the LORD's faithful love is from forever ago to forever from now for those who honor him. And God's righteousness reaches to the grandchildren of those who keep his covenant and remember to keep his commands.
Psalm 103:17-18

Excerpt from *River's End*, Chapter 24

"*D*id you see Mrs. Smyth today?" Sarah asked. . . . "She came by to tell me that I'd been accepted at the university."

"*Really?*" Anna blinked. She'd almost forgotten that Mrs. Smyth had been helping Sarah to apply to some local colleges.

Sarah grinned. "So I guess it's final. I'll be going to the U of O this fall. I think I want to major in anthropology or sociology . . . or something like that."

"Oh, sweetheart, Hazel would be so proud of you."

Sarah shook her head with an amazed expression. "It's still kind of hard to believe. I mean when I think about where I was at . . . just last fall. Pretty weird."

"You've come a long way."

She nodded, calling out a cheery greeting to an older couple who'd just come into the store. "What a trip, huh?"

Several more customers came into the store now and Anna knew that Sarah needed to give them her attention. So, congratulating her on the college acceptance, Anna left. But as she walked up to the house, she felt an unexpected sadness come over her. Oh, certainly, it was bittersweet . . . but it was still there. Sarah would be leaving in the fall. Once again, she would be removed from Anna's life. And, really, Anna wouldn't have it any other way. Sarah was too brilliant not to continue her education. And to think she was interested in the same things Hazel had studied and taught; well, it was beyond wonderful. Still, it would be hard to say goodbye . . . again.

Even so, Anna put on a happy face when she told Clark about Sarah's good news that evening. Sarah had gone to town with some of the other workers, to take in a movie. Naturally, Clark was pleased to hear that Sarah wanted to follow in his mother's footsteps. "I knew she'd been reading Mom's work, but I figured it had more to do with your family's history. I didn't realize she was actually interested in the field herself.

Good for her."

"It's going to be hard to see her go," Anna admitted.

He made a sympathetic smile. "Your old friend—change—is back again."

She felt silly. "I know…everything has to keep changing." She looked out over the river from the upper deck where they were having coffee. "Even this river, which I think of as changeless is constantly changing. Otherwise it would become stagnant and sick. New water is always coming from the mountains and then off it goes out to the sea…never the same water…it keeps moving…keeps it healthy."

"Just like the workers and family and friends that flow through here," Clark said. "They come and they go."

She reached for his hand. "But you're still here."

He smiled, nodded. "You bet I am."

"Even this river, which I think of as changeless is constantly changing. Otherwise it would become stagnant and sick. New water is always coming from the mountains and then off it goes out to the sea . . . keeps it healthy."

• • • • • • •

DAY 1: THE WINDS OF CHANGE

Read God's Word

"Everybody who hears these words of mine and puts them into practice is like a wise builder who built a house on bedrock. The rain fell, the floods came, and the wind blew and beat against that house. It didn't fall because it was firmly set on bedrock. But everybody who hears these words of mine and doesn't put them into practice will be like a fool who built a house on sand. The rain fell, the floods came, and the wind blew and beat against that house. It fell and was completely destroyed."

Matthew 7:24-27

Reflect and Respond

Just as the weather that destroyed the foolish builder's house came suddenly and unexpectedly, so the winds of change blow suddenly and unexpectedly into our lives. Often it feels as though we are slaves to change. Just as we get to a place in our lives when we feel like we're in control, when we have it figured out, when we get comfortable—boom!—everything changes.

How do you feel about change? Are you a person who gets restless and needs to keep moving and changing your routine? Or do you like stability and get nervous about change?

154

How do you normally react when you are forced into change?

What are some things in your life that are changing right now? How do you feel about what's happening?

Often change can be an agent in our lives, pushing us into new situations and circumstances that ultimately prove to be beneficial. Have you found this to be true in your life? Why or why not?

In *River's End,* we find Anna's life in a constant state of change and adjustment. Sarah is lost and then returns, only to leave again. Lauren is in and out of the inn, moving away to go back to school. Hazel, a mother figure to Anna, passes away. The inn's support staff turns over each year as the workers' circumstances change. The inn grows and evolves, and the needs of the patrons keep changing. Anna is weary from all of the change happening around her. She longs for security and stability and struggles to cope with what seems like an ever-changing life. It seems as if the only things Anna can count on are Clark, the river, and her faith, constants in an ever-changing world.

In the Gospels, we see Jesus traveling from place to place, preaching to crowds of people and teaching them about the ways of God. In today's passage from Matthew 7, we find Jesus teaching a parable about a wise builder. Reread the verses again now.

In this parable, what does the bedrock represent?

What might the sand represent?

On what foundation are you building your life? Take a few moments to think about what you consider the foundation of your life. Is it family? Faith? Your own abilities? In whom or what are you trusting?

Though constant winds of change blow through our lives and the rains of adversity batter the roofs, God can be trusted to carry us through every storm.

When we place the foundation of our lives on the bedrock—on God—we build on that which is ancient and unmoving. God is the Creator and Author of all. God spoke the earth and the heavens into being. God set the stars in the sky. God presides over all. Though constant winds of change blow through our lives and the rains of adversity batter the roofs, God can be trusted to carry us through every storm.

Read Revelation 1:8. Who does God say He is? How can you take comfort in these words today?

Read Deuteronomy 31:6. What struggles are you marching through right now? Do you know that God is marching in step with you, right through the mess? How do you feel God's presence right now?

Talk to God

Almighty One, you are the beginning and the end, the one who was and is and is to come. I praise you for your unchanging nature. You are my rock, Lord, and I know that you can carry me through whatever challenges and changes this life has to offer. Help me to trust in your surety and to move forward knowing that your grace holds me up. Amen.

As You Go

What changes and challenges in your life may be pushing you toward a new beginning? How does the possibility of a new beginning make you feel? Hopeful? Scared? Bring your emotions and fears to God today, asking for comfort and guidance, and then claim His promise in Psalm 103:17: "But the LORD's faithful love is from forever ago to forever from now for those who honor him."

DAY 2: A TIME TO LET GO

Read God's Word

There's a season for everything and a time for every matter under the heavens: . . . a time for searching and a time for losing, a time for keeping and a time for throwing away.

Ecclesiastes 3:1, 6

Reflect and Respond

From the moment that Anna comes back to the river in *River's Song,* she feels as if she is finally home. Having lived in Pine Ridge for more than twenty years and having rarely visited the river during that time, her first moments of stepping back onto her parents' property are filled with relief and regret, anxiety and anticipation. Though at first it is hard for Anna to imagine having a different life, being on the river gives her a new hope for her life that she hadn't dared to dream of. Though unexpected and somewhat frightening, this new hope burrows into Anna's heart and grows, fed by the beauty around her and by those who recognize her true gifting. This love and hope gives Anna the strength to begin anew, and we see her transformation continuing through each of the novels in the series.

In order to begin a new life, Anna had to let go of her life in Pine Ridge. Why do you think Anna stayed on in Pine Ridge even after Adam's death?

How did those years shape her life?

Ultimately Anna found herself by returning to the river. Do you think there are reasons that we learn more about ourselves when we return to the places of our youth? Why or why not?

What physical place do you consider "home"? What do you associate with that place? How do you feel when you are there?

Today's Scripture reminds us that there is a time for everything. Ecclesiastes 3:6 tells us there is "a time for keeping and a time for throwing away."

During her time in Eunice's house, Anna was essentially the housekeeper and cook for the family, scrutinized under Eunice's watchful eye and subject to her hurtful verbal abuse. This was her life for many years, and one that subdued and crushed her spirit until she couldn't imagine a different life. But though it certainly was not her ideal life, it was the only life she knew, and she held on to that life until her mother's death brought her back to the river and beckoned her to dream once again. For Anna, "throwing away" her old life for a new one—shaking off the years that left her subdued and broken—took courage and determination and, above all, trust.

Through faith in Jesus' sacrifice, we are made new and given new lives and new purposes by God. God has given us a new beginning and walks with us in every step of that new life.

For most of us, letting something go is a fearful process. Why do you think that is so? What do you think is behind that fear?

What might you need to let go of in order to open yourself up to something new?

Second Corinthians 5:17 is a celebration of letting go—and of embracing (or "keeping") the renewed, transformed life we have in Christ. Read the following Scripture versions of this verse. Circle the one that speaks most powerfully to you:

So then, if anyone is in Christ, that person is part of the new creation. The old things have gone away, and look, new things have arrived! (CEB)

Now we look inside, and what we see is that anyone united with the Messiah gets a fresh start, is created new. The old life is gone; a new life burgeons! (*THE MESSAGE*)

Therefore if anyone is in Christ, he is a new creature; the old things passed away; behold, new things have come. (NASB)

So if anyone is in Christ, there is a new creation: everything old has passed away; see, everything has become new! (NRSV)

Through faith in Jesus' sacrifice, we are made new and given new lives and new purposes by God. God has given us a new beginning and walks with us in every step of that new life.

Do you think you might be holding yourself back from a new beginning God may be offering you? If so, what are some reasons for that, and how can you open yourself up to God's leading?

Talk to God

Lord, I praise you for being a God of renewal and transformation. Thank you for transforming my life and making me a new creature. Help me to clearly see my life—to recognize my own needs, as well as the needs of those around me. Help me know what to keep and what to let go so that you can fill me with all your good things. Attune my ears to your leading and give me courage to step out when you call. Amen.

As You Go

Read and meditate on 1 Corinthians 2:9. Take some time to pray and dream about what God might be preparing for you.

Day 3: Hope in the Wait

Read God's Word

"Wait for the Lord; *be strong, and let your heart take courage; wait for the* Lord*!"*
Psalm 27:14

Reflect and Respond

There are times in our lives when we do anything and everything but wait. And in our impatience and restlessness, we find ourselves running blind—fast and furious toward anything that might give us relief from the pain we are experiencing. Such was the case with Sarah when she left the river, running away from her family and the life she had known. When she finally returns two years later, she begins to open up to Anna about the journey she has been on.

Excerpt from *River's End,* Chapter 3

Seated across from her granddaughter in a well-worn easy chair, Anna turned the coffee mug around and around in her hands. . . . Anna could understand why Sarah had run away. First of all, Lauren had all but abandoned Sarah—possibly when Sarah needed her the most. It was true Lauren had been getting over her addiction to Valium and alcohol and that she'd been on the verge of a nervous breakdown, but in Sarah's eyes it must've felt like abandonment. And when Sarah's father embarked on a scandalous affair with his secretary...

"Everyone felt so sorry for me," Sarah continued. "They welcomed me and made me feel at home." She looked at Anna with misty eyes. "Besides being here with you and Clark and Hazel, that was the closest thing to home I'd ever experienced. And I loved it . . . at first."

"What changed?" Anna asked gently. She was eager to hear Sarah's entire story, where she'd been and who she'd been with, but up until now Sarah had been closed tighter than a freshly dug razor clam about the past two years.

Sarah leaned back in the old rocker, pushing her fingers through the loopholes in the knitted afghan over her lap. It was one that Anna's mother had crocheted many years ago. "Lots of things changed," she said slowly. "First of all, Aaron left. That was when it all started to go downhill."

"Aaron?"

Sarah looked out the window with a slightly dreamy expression. "Aaron was our leader. He was a truly good man. He loved God with his whole heart. And he wanted us to follow his example."

Anna was beginning to understand now. Sarah had probably been in one of the communes that had become so prolific in Oregon and California, especially along the coast. This particular phenomenon had started in the late sixties and had continued into the seventies. In fact, Anna even remembered a time when the inn had been suspected of being a commune of sorts. Of course, Anna had simply taken that in stride and eventually the ridiculous rumors faded.

"Aaron and Misty were like our spiritual parents," Sarah continued. "Everything they did was for our own good. Even when we didn't like their decisions, we knew they loved us. You could just feel it. Aaron and Misty were good people."

Anna just nodded.

"And for a while, everything was perfect."

"Perfect?" Anna tried not to sound too skeptical.

"Well . . . maybe not perfect. But it was good. Really good."

"I'm curious about something, Sarah…"

"What?"

"Why didn't you call us? Just to let us know you were all right. We were so worried about you. You were so young…and we had no idea what had happened."

Sarah seemed to consider this. "A condition of staying in the family was to break all outside ties. We were forbidden to contact anyone from our past."

"Oh…"

"But it's not like they forced us. We did it willingly," she said quickly. "It wasn't as if we were being held prisoner there." She frowned. "Well, not at first anyway."

"But later? Were you ever held against your will?"

Sarah took in a long slow breath, folding her arms in front of her, and Anna could tell that this was her way of communicating that she'd said too much. And, really, Anna had been trying not to prod. "So…Aaron…" Anna tried again. "It sounds like he was a good guy . . . and you say he treated you like family…?"

"Yes," she said cautiously.

"And Misty was his wife?"

Sarah shrugged. "We don't use those kinds of traditional words. It was very unconventional there. We were all brothers and sisters. But, yes, Aaron and Misty were together as a couple, if that's what you mean."

"How many people were in this, uh, family?" Anna asked gently.

"It varied. At the most, it was about a hundred, I think. By the time I left it had dwindled a lot. Maybe thirty or so. After Aaron and Misty left, everything just started to change. The family became something that wasn't what I was looking for."

"What were you looking for?"

"Peace…inner peace." She sighed sadly.

"And did you find it?"

Sarah looked out the window with a longing expression. "I thought I did…at first."

"But it didn't last?" Anna gently prodded.

Sarah just shook her head.

> I sometimes want to run ahead instead of waiting on God's timing. But I've learned, over the years, that it pays to wait. . . . Besides that, some surprisingly beautiful things can happen while we're waiting.

• • • • • • •

Sarah, wounded by her parents and desperately craving a new beginning, had been drawn into a group that promised love and devotion and care for her vulnerable state. Relying on her own wisdom, Sarah thought she had it all figured out. But soon she was disappointed and lost once again.

I can relate to Sarah's impatience. I know how I get overly eager for something to happen. I know how I sometimes want to run ahead instead of waiting on God's timing. But I've learned, over the years, that it pays to wait. I respect that God has seasons—both in nature and in our lives. And just like it's futile to rush my garden by planting annuals while it's still freezing at night, it's silly to rush through a door that God hasn't opened—

not to mention painful. Besides that, some surprisingly beautiful things can happen while we're waiting.

Read the following verses. What does each verse say about humanity's wisdom and the wisdom of God?

1 Corinthians 1:27

1 Corinthians 2:12

1 Corinthians 3:18-20

When you are restless and searching, desperate for a new beginning, run to the Lord and ask for divine counsel.

Scripture is clear that God's wisdom is far superior to any wisdom we humans can obtain or conjure up on our own. But, too often, in our haste to make things better or ease the pain, we act out of our own wisdom. We make hasty decisions and move before praying for God's leading hand to guide us.

How do you typically make important decisions in your life? Do you consult with your family and friends? Pray? Research all the options? Explain.

Practically speaking, how much is seeking God part of your decision-making process?

Are you ever afraid to seek God's will in your life? Why or why not?

When you are restless and searching, desperate for a new beginning, run to the Lord and ask for divine counsel. Today's Scripture reminds us, "Wait for the LORD; be strong, and let your heart take courage; wait for the LORD!" (Psalm 27:14 NRSV).

Waiting is not a concept that we grasp very well. In our super-speed hi-tech world, we rarely have to wait for anything—the world is seemingly at our fingertips every moment of the day. But God challenges us to wait expectantly for His voice and leading in our lives.

What do the following verses have to say about aspects of waiting on the Lord?

Lamentations 3:25

Psalm 130:5-6

Galatians 6:9

Psalm 46:10 says, "Be still, and know that I am God." What do you think it means to "be still"? How might you practice this in your own life?

Though the waiting may be difficult, God always shows up at the perfect time. God knows your situation and the cries of your heart, and God will not fail to lead you in the right way.

Talk to God

God, you know that it is hard for me to wait. You understand how I want to figure everything out and make it all work out perfectly. Thank you for reminding me that you have it all under control and that all I have to do is to keep my eyes on you. Help me to be still and to wait for you to bring about new beginnings and opportunities in my life. Lead me, Lord. I believe that you are good to me. Amen.

As You Go

Poet Elizabeth Barrett Browning wrote, "God's gifts put man's best dreams to shame." Have you found this to be true in your own life? Reflect on this today.

> Though the waiting may be difficult, God always shows up at the perfect time. God knows your situation and the cries of your heart, and God will not fail to lead you in the right way.

163

DAY 4: GOD GIVES GOOD THINGS

Read God's Word

Ask, and you will receive. Search, and you will find. Knock, and the door will be opened to you. For everyone who asks, receives. Whoever seeks, finds. And to everyone who knocks, the door is opened. Who among you will give your children a stone when they ask for bread? Or give them a snake when they ask for fish? If you who are evil know how to give good gifts to your children, how much more will your heavenly Father give good things to those who ask him.

Matthew 7:7-11

Reflect and Respond

Good things . . .

As a young girl, did you think your life would be filled with good things? What did you think your life would be like when you were "older"? Chances are you spent time daydreaming about what it would be like to be grown up and independent and fulfilling all your dreams. Maybe you were convinced that the cute guy in homeroom was destined to be your husband, or that your ability to write an outstanding essay was sure to lead to a career as a great journalist. No matter the dream, you were hopeful, expectant, and excited about the future.

Now that you are "older" and have lived some life and walked a few paths, do you still dream about your future, eager and expectant about what's around the next corner? If not, why? If so, what do you dream about?

> The gifts of wisdom and experience often come wrapped in pain and disappointment. . . . Too often we lose the wonder of life and forget how to look forward to the future with hope and expectation.

The gifts of wisdom and experience often come wrapped in pain and disappointment. As we experience life and all of its ups and downs, often our ability to dream gets lost in the shuffle. Instead of daydreaming about our futures and what God may have in store for us, we find ourselves focusing on the mistakes we've made in the past and the ways in which we've been jaded and disillusioned by the world. We lose that giddy excitement about what's next, thinking that we've already been there, done that, and it doesn't seem like much is left to do. Too often we lose the wonder of life and forget how to look forward to the future with hope and expectation.

Have you ever lost a dream or had it taken from you? What happened, and how has that affected your outlook on life, family, or career?

Do you believe, wherever you are in your life, that some new beginning is possible? Why or why not?

There's no doubt about it: the future is unknown and uncertain, and that can be a scary thing. But when we focus on the "maybes" and "what ifs" and "what nows" of life, we allow fear to bind and hold us back. Fear is a bully, bound on keeping us in our place and holding us back from experiencing the freedom of a life lived in Christ.

Read the following verses. What does God have to say about fear in each verse?

Psalm 27:1

John 14:27

2 Timothy 1:7

Fear breeds uncertainty in our lives and leads us to forget that we can rest in God's all-knowing care. We are God's children, and He holds our futures in His hands. Jesus told us to ask, search, and knock. And the assurance He gave us is that when we seek in this way, we will find not bad surprises but good gifts.

What does it mean to you that God will "give good things to those who ask him" (Matthew 7:11)?

> Jesus told us to ask, search, and knock. And the assurance He gave us is that when we seek in this way, we will find not bad surprises but good gifts.

God gives us the freedom to dream and explore while we wait expectantly for Him to move us toward wonderful things. Have you believed that God wants you to dream, and to dream big? Why or why not?

Hazel is a woman who knows how to dream, fulfilling her goals of getting her doctorate and becoming a college professor late in life—during a time in history when women didn't typically accomplish these things. Have you known someone like Hazel, a person who was willing to dream and then to act to make that happen? What about her (or his) life inspires you?

What healing needs to happen in your heart to give you the courage and faith to embark on a new beginning? How can you ask God, specifically, to work in your life to bring about that healing?

God has a dream for your life—first, that you would come to know and trust Him, and second, that you will walk with Him day by day. It is through this daily walk that God leads you into new experiences and journeys.

Talk to God

Lord God, I am amazed to know that you have a dream for my life, and that it is not limited to my own imagination. So often I am ruled by fear, God, and that fear stifles my hope and excitement about where you might be leading. Do not allow fear to take root in my heart, Lord, but help me to fix my eyes on you when I am afraid. Heal and strengthen my heart so that I am ready to hear your voice when you say, "Go!" Thank you for loving me and giving me such good things. Amen.

As You Go

God has a dream for your life—first, that you would come to know and trust Him, and second, that you will walk with Him day by day. It is through this daily walk that God leads you into new experiences and journeys of serving and celebrating the wonderful, unique ways God made you.

Do you desire a new dream for your life, a new adventure that God can lead you in? Spend some time in prayer today, asking for God to birth a new journey in your heart.

DAY 5: LIVING A PASSIONATE LIFE

Read God's Word

I consider everything a loss in comparison with the superior value of knowing Christ Jesus my LORD.

Philippians 3:8

Reflect and Respond

This passionate declaration was made by the Apostle Paul. Paul, author of many books in the New Testament, was a devoted follower of Christ and a prominent leader of the early Christian church. But that was after his life-changing encounter with Jesus on the road to Damascus.

Paul had quite a story to tell. Once a self-proclaimed enemy of Jesus Christ and his teachings, Paul (then called Saul) was the most unlikely candidate for a conversion, and yet God chose him, completely transforming Paul's life so that he could preach the good news of Christ. Even if you are familiar with his story, read it again as if reading it for the very first time.

> *Meanwhile, Saul was still spewing out murderous threats against the LORD's disciples. He went to the high priest, seeking letters to the synagogues in Damascus. If he found persons who belonged to the Way, whether men or women, these letters would authorize him to take them as prisoners to Jerusalem. During the journey, as he approached Damascus, suddenly a light from heaven encircled him. He fell to the ground and heard a voice asking him, "Saul, Saul, why are you harassing me?"*
>
> *Saul asked, "Who are you, LORD?"*
>
> *"I am Jesus, whom you are harassing," came the reply. "Now get up and enter the city. You will be told what you must do."*
>
> *Those traveling with him stood there speechless; they heard the voice but saw no one. After they picked Saul up from the ground, he opened his eyes but he couldn't see. So they led him by the hand into Damascus. For three days he was blind and neither ate nor drank anything.*
>
> *In Damascus there was a certain disciple named Ananias. The LORD spoke to him in a vision, "Ananias!" He answered, "Yes, LORD."*
>
> *The LORD instructed him, "Go to Judas' house on Straight Street and ask for a man from Tarsus named Saul. He is praying. In a vision he has seen a man named Ananias enter and put his hands on him to restore his sight."*

Ananias countered, "LORD, I have heard many reports about this man. People say he has done horrible things to your holy people in Jerusalem. He's here with authority from the chief priests to arrest everyone who calls on your name.

The LORD replied, "Go! This man is the agent I have chosen to carry my name before Gentiles, kings, and Israelites. I will show him how much he must suffer for the sake of my name."

Ananias went to the house. He placed his hands on Saul and said, "Brother Saul, the LORD sent me—Jesus, who appeared to you on the way as you were coming here. He sent me so that you could see again and be filled with the Holy Spirit." Instantly, flakes fell from Saul's eyes and he could see again. He got up and was baptized. After eating, he regained his strength.

He stayed with the disciples in Damascus for several days. Right away, he began to preach about Jesus in the synagogues. "He is God's Son," he declared.

Everyone who heard him was baffled. They questioned each other, "Isn't he the one who was wreaking havoc among those in Jerusalem who called on this name? Hadn't he come here to take those same people as prisoners to the chief priests?"

But Saul grew stronger and stronger. He confused the Jews who lived in Damascus by proving that Jesus is the Christ.

Acts 9:1-23

On the next Sabbath, almost everyone in the city gathered to hear the LORD's word. When the Jews saw the crowds, they were overcome with jealousy. They argued against what Paul was saying by slandering him. Speaking courageously, Paul and Barnabas said, "We had to speak God's word to you first. Since you reject it and show that you are unworthy to receive eternal life, we will turn to the Gentiles. This is what the LORD commanded us:

> *I have made you a light for the Gentiles,*
> *so that you could bring salvation*
> *to the end of the earth."*

When the Gentiles heard this, they rejoiced and honored the LORD's word. Everyone who was appointed for eternal life believed, and the LORD's word was broadcast throughout the entire region.

Acts 13:44-49

Paul, once an enemy, was now a favored child. He had a new name; he had a new identity. The Bible doesn't exactly tell us when or how Saul got a new name, only that he became known as Paul. Since God appointed Paul to minister to the Gentiles, perhaps God gave him the new name of Paul, a non-Jewish equivalent of his old name, so that he would be more approachable to the Gentiles. Maybe Paul chose the name for himself. Either way, Paul had a new name in which to live out his new identity.

Practically speaking, how might Paul's name change have affected his life? How can an individual's name define her or his life?

God delights in giving us new names and new identities as beloved children. Once Paul was called Enemy; God called him Chosen and Mine.

Maybe you've known yourself by other names too. Perhaps you've named yourself Broken. Not Enough. Worthless. But if you are a believer in Christ, God has changed your name. God calls you Lovely. Worthy. Beloved. God has already given you a new name and a new beginning. The moment you believed and were adopted into God's family, God gave you His name and His righteousness and a new beginning.

Just as our childhood nicknames no longer fit our adult lives, so we grow out of our old identities when we become children of God.

What name have you been living under that no longer fits you? Maybe you're struggling under the name of Unworthy or Stupid or Silly. Whatever the name, will you let go of it and let God give you a new name? What do you hear God calling you?

Once Paul got a new name and a new identity, he immediately began living a new life—one that was committed to preaching the good news of Christ and striving to know God more and more. His life was transformed in a dramatic new beginning, and from then on he lived passionately and wholeheartedly for God. He said,

The very credentials these people are waving around as something special, I'm tearing up and throwing out with the trash—along with everything else I used to take credit for. And why? Because of Christ. Yes, all the things I once thought were so important are gone from my life. Compared to the high privilege of knowing Christ Jesus as my Master, firsthand, everything I once thought I had going for me is insignificant— dog dung. I've dumped it all in the trash so that I could embrace Christ and be embraced by him. I didn't want some petty, inferior brand of righteousness that comes from keeping a list of rules when I could get the robust kind that comes from trusting Christ— God's righteousness.

Philippians 3:7-8 *THE MESSAGE*

What does it mean to live a passionate life? Are you a person who lives this way? If not, what do you think holds you back from living that kind of life?

When we know how much God has changed our lives, we want to know him more. Read Paul's words in the following verses. How does each passage speak to living a passionate, committed life?

Romans 6:3-14

Romans 8:28-29

Philippians 3:12-14

How can you passionately embrace the new beginning that God has already given you through the gift of salvation and your adoption as God's beloved child? What would this look like in your life?

How can you fearlessly pour yourself into the life God has given you? What holds you back? What encourages you?

Talk to God

Father, thank you that I can call you by that name—Father. I praise you for all you have done in my life and all that you are yet to do. You have exchanged my worthless righteousness for your perfect love, and I am so thankful. I want to know more about your goodness and your forgiveness so that I can proclaim those mercies to others. Help me to get rid of the hurtful names from my past and cling to the new names you give me. Help me to know that I am forgiven, loved, and whole through you. Amen.

As You Go

Though God's love is strong, our minds are often weak, and we need to remind each other of our new names in Christ. Is there someone in your life who needs to be reminded of his or her new name in Christ? How can you encourage that person today and remind her (or him) of God's mercy and love? Journal about the experience afterward (journaling pages are provided at the back of the book).

We need to remind each other of our new names in Christ.

VIDEO NOTES
A FEW MINUTES WITH MELODY

INTERESTING INSIGHTS:

POINTS I'D LIKE TO DISCUSS WITH THE GROUP:

WEEK 8
EXPERIENCING THE GOODNESS OF GOD

Scripture for the Week

Let my whole being bless the LORD!
Let everything inside me
bless his holy name!...
All you heavenly forces,
bless the LORD!
All you who serve him and do his will,
bless him!
All God's creatures,
bless the LORD!
Everywhere, throughout his kingdom,
let my whole being
bless the LORD!
Psalm 103:1, 21-22

Excerpt from *River's End,* Chapter 16

*H*azel looked into Anna's eyes. *"I want to thank you, Anna."*

"Thank me for what?"

"For allowing me to share this special place with you...for letting me be part of your life...for how you help others to forgive...and your healing touch...for showing us how to live in peace...thank you."

Anna didn't know what to say.

"You've given many of us a home, Anna. Sometimes for a few days...sometimes for many more. You've created a place that feels like a small portion of the heavenly home that's awaits us. For that I thank you."

Anna took Hazel's hand again, gently squeezing it. "Then I must thank you, too, Hazel."

Hazel looked surprised. "What for?"

"For coming here and befriending me. It was a very fragile time in my life...that day I met you on the river. I had no idea that you held so many keys."

"Keys?" Hazel's brows arched with interest.

"The key to my grandmother's stories, the key to my past, the key to my future."

Hazel waved a tired hand. "Oh, you're wrong about that. You already had those keys. All you had to do was to follow your heritage."

"But you helped me to see my heritage."

"It was already in you, Anna."

Anna shook her head. "Maybe it was there. But it was locked up. You had the key, Hazel. I thank you for that."

God's forgiveness heals and restores us, and God can help us extend that same grace and forgiveness to others—with powerful results.

· · · · · · · ·

Day 1: Leaning Into Forgiveness and Healing

As we enter into the last week of our study, we will review the things we've learned that will bring healing into our lives, and we will revel in God's promises to walk with us on our journey to healing.

Read God's Word

As far as east is from west—that's how far God has removed our sin from us.

Psalm 103:12

Reflect and Respond

Have you ever thought about how far the east is from the west? The distance cannot be measured, but the sentiment is clear—God's forgiveness and grace separate us completely from our sin. God's forgiveness heals and restores us, and God can help us extend that same grace and forgiveness to others—with powerful results. After many years of bitterness and unforgiveness on Sarah's part, Anna begins to wonder if Lauren and Sarah's mother-daughter relationship will ever be fully restored, until she sees the two walking together on Christmas morning.

Excerpt from *River's End,* Chapter 29

The next morning Anna got up early and was making coffee in the kitchen when she noticed two figures down by the river. It was hard to tell who they were since it was barely dawn and a thick blanket of fog had rolled onto the riverbank overnight. But they appeared to be embracing. Probably one of the couples sharing a Christmas hug. But then as the pair walked up to the house, Anna nearly fell over from shock. Blinking to see if her eyes were playing tricks, she realized it was really true—Lauren and Sarah, mother and daughter, walking side by side on their way up to the house.

Anna took in a deep breath and waited for the front door to open and then, trying not to look as stunned as she felt, welcomed them, casually offering them coffee.

"Oh, Grandma," Sarah said in a teasing tone. "Don't pretend you're not shocked by the fact that Mom and I are acting civilly."

Anna poured three cups. "Well, I'll admit you've caught me off guard."

"I went to talk to Sarah last night," Lauren explained. "But then, for some reason, I decided not to. Instead, I went to bed early. Then this morning, I woke early and went for a walk. When I saw Sarah down on the dock, I thought I'd corner her. I marched down there thinking I'd force her to listen to my full apology. Either that or she'd have to jump into the river." Lauren laughed. "But I'd barely asked her to forgive me and she said yes. Just like that!"

"Actually, there's a little more to it than that." Sarah took a cup and sat down at the kitchen table. "I was feeling guilty."

"Guilty?" Anna sat down across from her.

"Yes. I was thinking about Christmas—I mean that it's supposed to be the celebration of Jesus Christ's birth—and I remembered the Bible verses you told me to read, before Grandpa got hurt."

"About forgiveness?"

Sarah nodded. "I read them yesterday morning."

"Good for you."

"And I'd been thinking about them off and on all day. Then last night when everyone was having a good time together and I realized how miserable I was . . . that's why I left."

"So she could be miserable alone," Lauren said in a slightly teasing tone. Then she smiled apologetically at Sarah and sat down. "Sorry. But I'm glad you took the time to think about it. Not just for my sake either." She sighed. "When I think how long it took me to figure these things out—well, maybe I still am—anyway, you're way ahead of me."

Sarah looked at Anna with sparkling eyes. "So, I kept thinking about everything you'd said. And I read those verses again. It was around midnight when it started to make sense. I started to figure it out—and it just hit me. I finally got it."

"About forgiveness?"

"Yes!" She smiled happily. "I understood that I was blocking God from forgiving me when I refused to forgive my mom. I could see how I'd built this wall all around me.

"I understood that I was blocking God from forgiving me when I refused to forgive my mom. I could see how I'd built this wall all around me. Each stone was like each time I chose not to forgive. I realized how this wall isolated me from God and from others . . . And I knew I needed to knock it down."

Each stone was like each time I chose not to forgive. I realized how this wall isolated me from God and from others—and that it was making me miserable. And I knew I needed to knock it down. And that's what I did."

"We both happened to get up early," Lauren told Anna. "To go for a walk." She winked. "Think that was a coincidence?"

"I think God planned the whole thing," Anna said with certainty.

"As soon as I saw Sarah, I started telling her how sorry I was about everything—but she cut me off. She didn't even let me apologize for all the messes I've put her through over the years." Lauren shook her head. "And it was a long, long list."

"But I didn't really need to hear it anymore," Sarah confessed.

Anna could hardly believe her ears.

"Because I had already forgiven her." Sarah smiled at her mother.

"Good for you," Anna reached for Sarah's hand and then for Lauren's. "Good for both of you."

"I'll say." Lauren sighed. "What a relief."

"You were right all along, Grandma," Sarah admitted sheepishly. "And I feel so much better now. I don't know why I couldn't see it before."

"It doesn't matter," Anna assured her. "What's important is that you see it now. What a wonderful Christmas present for you, Sarah. And for all of us."

. . . .

As the Inn at Shining Waters Series so aptly illustrates, forgiveness is a beautiful thing. Not only is it a restorative, cleansing act; it is one that is necessary for our spiritual health and well-being.

As we studied in week 2, our God is devoted to reconciliation and restoration. Jesus came to earth to die for the sins of the world. He took our sin, placed it on His perfect shoulders, and bore the burden of payment for our sins. Through Jesus, God bestowed His forgiveness and righteousness on us, and as Psalm 103:12 tells us, He flung our sins away—as far as the east is from the west!

When you think about the complete and perfect forgiveness that God has extended to you, what reaction is birthed in your heart? What does it move you to do?

> Forgiveness is a beautiful thing. Not only is it a restorative, cleansing act; it is one that is necessary for our spiritual health and well-being.

Read again the story Jesus tells in Matthew 18:21–35 (you first read this story in Day 4 of Week 2). What strikes you most about this story?

Time and time again in Scripture, God tells us to forgive *as we have been forgiven*. When we are able to wholeheartedly accept Christ's redemption and free grace given to us, we receive a strength we never believed possible. We are free to be generous and lavish others with forgiveness, knowing that God is the one in charge. Like Anna, we can find the strength to offer forgiveness to others, even when they don't ask for it.

Because we have been so fully and graciously forgiven, God calls us to forgive others generously and completely. And that's not always easy. As we saw in week 2, it's important to realize that forgiveness is a process, one that often doesn't come quickly and easily. Forgiveness involves making a choice to continually offer up our hurt and disappointment to our Creator, asking for the help to forgive over and over again. When old hurts and resentments surface, we need to come to Him again and again, perhaps day after day, asking for the strength to forgive and let go.

Perhaps the coming-to and asking-of Jesus is the greatest element to our healing. When, in our weakness and bitterness, we are drawn to Him day after day, asking for healing and strength, we are building our dependence on Him and learning to trust Him more and more.

> Forgiveness involves making a choice to continually offer up our hurt and disappointment to our Creator, asking for the help to forgive over and over again.

Read Proverbs 3:5-6. What do you think it means to trust in the Lord "with all your heart"?

When you draw from your own strength, what do you tend to rely on the most? Your intelligence? Your emotions? Your reasoning? Your abilities? Something else?

Have you ever encountered something or someone that you could not handle in your own strength? What happened? How did you feel? Where did you turn for help?

Read Psalm 51:10. How does the work of forgiveness cleanse our hearts and give us a faithful spirit?

Leaning into forgiveness means leaning into God for support and healing.

When we ask for help, God will heal our hearts and release us from the weight of bitterness and anger. We can show up, ask God for help, and obey His leading, but God does the work of forgiveness in our hearts. And when we experience this forgiveness, we are freed to live our lives fully and openly. Our load will be lighter, and like the psalmist, we can proclaim, "Let my whole being bless the Lord! Let everything inside me bless his holy name!" (Psalm 103:1).

In The Inn at Shining Waters Series, which character's journey to forgiveness do you most relate to, and why?

What have you learned about forgiveness from this study?

Is there anything that God is calling you to do, specifically, to right a wrong or offer forgiveness to someone in your life? Explain.

Talk to God

Forgiving God, thank you for your complete forgiveness and love for me. Thank you for working forgiveness in my life. Help me to come to you with my bitterness and anger and hurt and allow you to transform that into something beautiful that glorifies you. Amen.

As You Go

Leaning into forgiveness means leaning into God for support and healing. Where do you need to lean in to God today?

DAY 2: DIVING INTO GRACE

Read God's Word

I'm holding back from bragging so that no one will give me any more credit than what anyone sees or hears about me. I was given a thorn in my body because of the outstanding revelations I've received so that I wouldn't be conceited. It's a messenger from Satan sent to torment me so that I wouldn't be conceited. I pleaded with the LORD three times for it to leave me alone. He said to me, "My grace is enough for you, because power is made perfect in weakness." So I'll gladly spend my time bragging about my weaknesses so that Christ's power can rest on me.

2 Corinthians 12:6-10

Reflect and Respond

The Apostle Paul was a big shot in certain circles. Travelling extensively, boldly preaching the gospel of Christ, and mentoring members of the early Christian churches, Paul was sought after by those wanting to know more about Jesus, and churches hung on his every word. With all the notoriety Paul was getting, it certainly would have been easy for him to feel proud about all the work he was accomplishing.

But Paul refused to brag. Not only that, he admitted to having a "thorn"—some unnamed limitation—that tormented him. We are never told what Paul's "thorn" was—perhaps it was a character flaw that he struggled with, or a habitual sin that he often fought with and lost. Paul was human, just like us, so it's not hard to imagine that he struggled with a myriad of issues that frustrated and discouraged him. His fallen human nature alone could have been enough to torment him. Whatever Paul battled with, his struggles showed other believers that Paul was flawed, and that he too was in need of a savior.

We aren't too fond of flaunting our weaknesses, are we? In a world where it seems that only the strongest thrive, we are encouraged to always put forth our best efforts and to hide any areas of weakness, lest they be used against us and exploited. For the

We don't have to be afraid to be vulnerable and honest about our shortcomings because through those weaknesses God is given praise.

believer, this means that sometimes we tend to act like we have it all together, that we are in control of our sin and making great strides toward holiness. But in this scenario, who is given the praise? The individual receives praise, not God.

We don't have to be afraid to be vulnerable and honest about our shortcomings because through those weaknesses God is given praise. It allows us to say, "I haven't done anything good on my own—it is Christ working through me." His grace shines through, not our flawed efforts.

How do you feel about celebrating your weaknesses? Is that something you typically tend to do? Why or why not?

When you discover a weakness in yourself, what do you do? Try to fix it? Hide in shame? Confide in someone else? How do you handle it?

What might it look like, practically, for you to "brag" about your weaknesses and to proclaim God's strength—not in a way that is falsely humble, but in a way that points others to God?

Do you have a "thorn" that you have been asking God to take away from you? How is God answering that prayer? Are you accepting the answer?

We proclaim God's strength and mercy and grace because it is the only thing that can penetrate our hearts and minds and truly transform our lives. Jesus said "the kingdom of heaven is like yeast, which a woman took and hid in a bushel of wheat flour until the yeast had worked its way through all the dough" (Matthew 13:33). When mixed into flour, yeast works its way through every bit of dough so that the dough will rise when baked. In the same way, when we receive God's grace, it works its way through our lives and hearts, permeating every bit of us. We can't see it working, but it is permeating every nook and cranny. It is a slow and gradual process that takes time, but it moves all the same.

God faithfully works grace through us, thoroughly refining us. Though the process often seems slow, God isn't worried or rushed. God has the time, knows the plan, and will patiently finish the work.

Read Mark 4:26-29. How does this parable relate to the parable about the yeast?

How does it feel to know that God's work in your life will primarily be a gradual process? Does that frustrate or encourage you? Why?

During the course of this study, in what ways have you noticed God's grace working its way through your life, permeating the nooks and crannies of your heart?

God faithfully works grace through us, thoroughly refining us. Though the process often seems slow . . . God has the time, knows the plan, and will patiently finish the work.

The Lord isn't in a hurry and never fails to give us what we need. It doesn't matter when the sun sets and rises, when one day ends and another begins. God never changes. For every day of our lives, God is enough:

> *"Certainly the faithful love of the LORD hasn't ended; certainly God's compassion isn't through! They are renewed every morning. Great is your faithfulness. I think: The LORD is my portion! Therefore, I'll wait for him."*
> Lamentations 3:22-24

In your journey of healing, how has God shown you that He is enough for you? How has God protected you and equipped you and encouraged you to dive into His grace?

Talk to God

God of Grace, every day you provide for me and walk with me on this journey. In all that I say, and in all that I do, I pray that you would be glorified, Lord. Thank you for the gift of your unending grace and mercy. May I be willing—eager, even—to brag about my own weaknesses and to point others toward you. Amen.

183

As You Go

God is strong when we are weak, and we can count on Him to protect and provide for us every day of our lives. Read Ephesians 6:10-18. How does this passage encourage us to claim God's grace every day? How will you respond to the instruction found in these verses today?

> God is strong when we are weak, and we can count on Him to protect and provide for us every day of our lives.

DAY 3: TRUSTING IN THE LORD

Read God's Word

"Are you tired? Worn out? Burned out on religion? Come to me. Get away with me and you'll recover your life. I'll show you how to take a real rest. Walk with me and work with me—watch how I do it. Learn the unforced rhythms of grace. I won't lay anything heavy or ill-fitting on you. Keep company with me and you'll learn to live freely and lightly."

Matthew 11:28-30 *THE MESSAGE*

Reflect and Respond

When we walk with Jesus, we pray for His grace to flow naturally and freely into our lives. Though the tides of Anna's life, and the life of the Inn at Shining Waters, seem to be ever-changing as each season comes and goes, Anna knows that she can rely on God's grace as a source of constant nourishment and support.

Excerpt from *River's End*, Chapter 26

As usual, Anna had mixed feelings when Labor Day arrived. On one hand, she was relieved that their busiest time of year was coming to an end . . . but at the same time, it was hard to say goodbye to another summer. And it had been such a pleasant one—not only because of Sarah's being with them, but the weather had been delightful too. Sunny and mild and, other than that sorrowful time of the dying whales in June, it had been a perfect summer.

Even so, the hardest part about seeing it end was knowing Sarah was about to leave for school. Sometimes Anna wondered how many more times of partings she could bear. Oh, certainly, it was a part of life...but why was it that it seemed to grow more difficult as one grew older? Was this how her mother had felt when Anna had married and left so many decades ago?

Not for the first time, Anna wondered about how it had been a hundred years ago...or back before the white man came. Back in a slower time...when families and communities stayed together, helping each other, living peaceably alongside the river ...and no one left. Was that what she was always longing for? That sense of connectedness ...of being part of something bigger?

Anna continued to find comfort in the constancy of the river. Oh, yes, it was constantly changing as well. Always renewing itself, never running dry, it kept on flowing, even after a long warm summer, it didn't run out. Going and flowing, the Siuslaw rippled past the inn, shimmering like diamonds during the high tide, and always finding its way out to the sea. She could count on that in the same way that she could count on God's grace to continue to flow through her life.

In the midst of all the change in her life, Anna found comfort in the constancy of the river—and the constancy of God's presence and grace, which flowed freely like the Siuslaw. Like Anna's life, all of our lives here on earth are inextricably bound to change (also discussed in Day 1 of Week 7). Days turn into nights. Seasons come and go. Children grow. Jobs change. Friends move away. Wrinkles deepen. New relationships are formed. Change is a given of life.

What physical or environmental changes are you dealing with right now in your life?

What changes are happening in your heart?

When things are changing all around you, what do you tend to hold on to? What or who are the constants in your life?

Though change is inevitable, we can always count on the constancy of God and rely on the truth that God never changes. Scripture tells us this.

> "Going and flowing, the Siuslaw rippled past the inn ... always finding its way out to the sea. She could count on that in the same way that she could count on God's grace to continue to flow through her life."

Read the following verses. Beneath each verse, write one word that describes the nature of God.

Jesus Christ is the same yesterday, today, and forever!
Hebrews 13:8

"I the LORD do not change."
Malachi 3:6 NIV

God isn't a man that he would lie, or a human being that he would change his mind. Has he ever spoken and not done it, or promised and not fulfilled it?

Numbers 23:19

Every good and perfect gift is from above, coming down from the Father of the heavenly lights, who does not change like the shifting shadows.
James 1:17 NIV

We women tend to feel we need to do it all . . . No wonder we are so weary. . . . Jesus calls out to us to come to Him.

Change can be scary, stressful, and exciting. Often when change comes along, our natural inclination is to try to somehow control it, to manipulate it into something we can understand and handle. We easily forget that God is ancient and strong, able to speak wisdom into the changing tides of our lives.

Many women work long hours each day to meet an endless list of demands that they consider to be simply the basics: working in and out of the home, caring for the needs of family and community, and striving to have a devoted spiritual life. Others enjoy going above and beyond when they are able–cooking gourmet meals, decorating brilliantly, serving in dynamic ministries–the list is endless. No wonder we are so weary. Our quest for keeping everything under control and getting it done right is stifling our spirits and clouding our hearts. Jesus calls out to us to come to Him. Reread His words once again, taking them in thoughtfully and carefully:

"Are you tired? Worn out? Burned out on religion? Come to me. Get away with me and you'll recover your life. I'll show you how to take a real rest. Walk with me and work with me—watch how I do it. Learn the unforced rhythms of grace. I won't lay anything heavy or ill-fitting on you. Keep company with me and you'll learn to live freely and lightly."

Matthew 11:28-30 *THE MESSAGE*

What parts of this passage speak to your heart today?

Do you have trouble letting go of certain aspects in your life? In what areas do you find yourself most wanting to control?

How might your desire to make things manageable and controlled stifle your ability to trust God?

When God calls us into service, He enables us to handle the call and brings others alongside us.

God is able to reign over every aspect of our lives and is willing and eager to take the burden of both our present and our future off our shoulders. Will you rely on God and trust God's path for your life?

Talk to God

Lord, I praise you for the truth that you never change. Thank you for being willing today—and tomorrow—to walk with me and show me your goodness and love. Help me to recognize the areas in my life that I am so desperate to control, and enable me to get beneath that desire to uncover what's really going on in my heart. Help me to rest in you and in your promises through the changing seasons of my life. Amen.

As You Go

Reflect on these words from the old hymn "'Tis So Sweet to Trust in Jesus." In what areas of your life can you take Jesus at His word today?

> 'Tis so sweet to trust in Jesus
> Just to take Him at His Word
> Just to rest upon His promise
> And to know, "Thus saith the Lord!"
> Jesus, Jesus, how I trust Him!
> How I've proved Him o'er and o'er.
> Jesus, Jesus, precious Jesus,
> Oh, for grace to trust Him more!
> (Louisa M. R. Stead)

DAY 4: CELEBRATING OUR RELATIONSHIPS

One of the greatest blessings that life has to offer is the joy of journeying along with our friends and fellow believers. Though we sometimes trip and stumble along the way, we have others to support us and help us up. These relationships aren't just a blessing—they are a necessity. We need each other on this journey.

Read God's Word

We need others to fight for us, to pray for us, and to hold us up when we are weary.

Amalek came and fought with Israel at Rephidim. Moses said to Joshua, "Choose some men for us and go fight with Amalek. Tomorrow I'll stand on top of the hill with the shepherd's rod of God in my hand." So Joshua did as Moses told him. He fought with Amalek while Moses, Aaron, and Hur went up to the top of the hill. Whenever Moses held up his hand, Israel would start winning the battle. Whenever Moses lowered his hand, Amalek would start winning. But Moses' hands grew tired. So they took a stone and put it under Moses so he could sit down on it. Aaron and Hur held up his hands, one on each side of him so that his hands remained steady until sunset. So Joshua defeated Amalek and his army with the sword.

Exodus 17:8-13

Reflect and Respond

When God calls us into service, he enables us to handle the call and brings others alongside us. In Exodus 17 the Jews were being attacked. Joshua was called to fight, and Moses was called to pray. When Moses' uplifted hands, heavy with prayer, became weary and threatened to fall, Aaron and Hur were there to support him. Physically holding up his arms, one on either side, these men gave support and companionship to their fellow warrior during his battle.

We need others to fight for us, to pray for us, and to hold us up when we are weary. We need each other on this journey, and God blesses us with fellowship and encouragement from these brave warrior-friends along the way.

Read Galatians 6:2. Is there someone who needs you to hold up her (or his) arms right now? How can you support someone who is tired and weary from the fight? Spend some time in prayer over this question, asking God to reveal to you how you can serve others well. Make some notes below about what God reveals to you.

How does the relationship between Anna and Clark illustrate this picture of support and fighting for one another? In what other relationships in this series is this companionship illustrated?

Where do you need someone to step into your life today and hold up your arms? Name it.

Are you able to ask for help? Why do you think it's often hard to ask for help?

We need other believers to point us to God and remind us of who we are in Christ and how God has uniquely gifted each of us for this journey we are on.

When I was a new mother, I helped to lead a Bible study group for other young moms. For eight years, I was blessed with this group of lovely women. Together we encouraged each other to follow God wholeheartedly, and to love and serve our families. We even helped each other with daily tasks like cooking, gardening, and childcare. If a woman was sick or had a new baby, we took her family meals. These women were like my tribe, and I don't know how I would've made it through those early years of marriage and child rearing without them. And now, although we've moved a hundred miles away and my tribe has changed, they are just as valuable to me. God knows that we can see ourselves better through the eyes of our loved ones.

Read the following verses. What does each verse have to say about walking with others in our lives?

1 Thessalonians 5:11

Romans 12:10

Romans 1:11-12

Hebrews 3:13

We long for what is good. . . . We want the story to have a good ending–for goodness to reign. How wonderful that our desire for goodness is fulfilled in God!

How has this study encouraged you in your relationships?

You can't be everything to every person all the time, but you can give what you have. What special gifts and talents do you bring to your relationships? How can you encourage and serve others with what you have to give?

When things get sticky or difficult in your relationships, what encourages you to keep them strong?

How do your friends encourage and challenge you to live a life devoted to God? Maybe it's through humor or availability or loyalty or affirming words. Make a list below. Then give thanks for the people God has placed in your life.

Talk to God

God, you did not intend for me to make my journey alone. Thank you for the people you have brought into my life to share my hopes, dreams, hurts, and disappointments.

Though you are enough, you know that I need accountability and encouragement and sometimes a shoulder to cry on. Help me to remember how important my relationships are, God, and how I can best serve these children of yours with whom I share this road of life. Amen.

As You Go

Today, pray that the Lord would bring someone to mind—perhaps it's a friend, a coworker, a family member—and reveal to you a way you can love that person today. Then act—make the phone call, send a text, stop by to say hello. Pray that you would be a beautiful instrument for God's purposes today.

DAY 5: KNOWING THAT GOD IS GOOD

Read God's Word

No doubt about it! God is good.
Psalm 73:1

Reflect and Respond

Evangelist Billy Graham once said, "Man has two great spiritual needs. One is for forgiveness. The other is for goodness."[3]

We long for what is good. Consider the fairy tales we read as children. In each story there are the same elements, which basically boil down to good versus evil. We long for Cinderella to escape the grasp of the wicked stepmother. We cheer when the Big Bad Wolf cannot huff and puff his way through the little pigs' brick house. We want the story to have a good ending—for goodness to reign.

How wonderful that our desire for goodness is fulfilled in God! Scripture teaches us that God *is* good—not in the sense that goodness is one of his characteristics; rather, it is his *identity*. God is goodness itself.

Sometimes I'm amazed at God's goodness in my life. Sure, I've had some hard challenges along the way. Who hasn't? But most of the time I can't believe how blessed I am. I truly believe the best blessings are the simple ones, such as waking up to a sunny day, my husband handing me a cup of coffee, a walk with my dog in the woods. I see all these as God's good gifts—and I remind myself to be thankful!

Read the verses below and list how each describes the goodness of God.

Psalm 52:1

Psalm 136:1

1 John 1:5

No matter our circumstance or season in life, we can rest in the knowledge that God is good and does work goodness in all things for those who love Him, even when we can't see it.

God's goodness is displayed in creation—in the rolling hills and mountain peaks, in the songs of the birds, and in the cries of a newborn baby.

Read Genesis 1:31. How does creation speak to you of God's goodness?

Read Psalm 139:1-18. How do you see God's goodness in how He created you?

What do you think it means that God is good?

No matter our circumstance or season in life, we can rest in the knowledge that God is good and does work goodness in all things for those who love Him, even when we can't see it.

Read Psalm 73. How does the psalmist's perspective on God's goodness change from the beginning of the psalm to the end?

Often our definition of good means that we don't suffer, that we aren't poor or hungry, that we will be healthy, that we will be happy. Asaph, the author of Psalm 73, certainly felt that way. In the beginning of the psalm, he was angry that the godless seemed to be enjoying all the good things in life—wealth, happiness, power—while he was not. He was angry and bitter until he realized that God had not abandoned him but was walking with him day by day, and that God's justness would reign. Asaph's definition of good changed: "It's good for me to be near God. I have taken my refuge in you, my LORD God" (v. 28). Asaph realized that close fellowship with God—with goodness—was what was best.

Experiencing God's goodness in our lives doesn't always mean that things will be easy or perfect. When you have experienced hardship in your life, did you consider it "good"? Did you feel abandoned by God or did you feel God at work in your life?

How might having a correct biblical definition of good change our perspective on God?

Read Philippians 3:10. How can our sufferings become blessings?

Read Romans 8:28. Do you know that God is working for the good in your life, in every circumstance? How has God worked for the good in your life in the past? And how might God be doing that right now?

James 1:17 proclaims, "Every good gift, every perfect gift, comes from above. These gifts come down from the Father, the creator of the heavenly lights, in whose character there is no change at all."

Because God doesn't change, we can celebrate the God who doesn't give up, who delights in giving us new beginnings and lavishes us with good and perfect gifts. God heals us, restores us, and fills us with His unending grace. God has walked with you every step of your journey, and He will never leave you. Hallelujah!

> Experiencing God's goodness in our lives doesn't always mean that things will be easy or perfect.

Talk to God

Heavenly Father, you are good. I praise you for your goodness and how you work it in my life. When difficulties in life cause me to wonder about your goodness, come for me and remind me that you are working good in all you do in my life. Let my lips sing your praise! Amen.

As You Go

As you wrap up this study and your time in these novels, consider how God has been working in your heart. How is God working healing in your life? How has He spoken to you through this study? Describe your journey over the past eight weeks, as well as how you desire for God to continue working in your life. Then write a heartfelt prayer, expressing your gratitude and your commitment to God. If you need more space, use the journaling pages provided at the back of the book.

END NOTES

1. This theory was first introduced by Elisabeth Kübler-Ross in her 1969 publication, *On Death and Dying* (New York: Simon and Schuster).
2. Max Lucado, *And the Angels Were Silent* (Nashville: Thomas Nelson, 2004), 36.
3. Billy Graham, *The Holy Spirit: Activating God's Power in Your Life* (place of publication not available, 1988), p. xi.

VIDEO NOTES
A FEW MINUTES WITH MELODY

INTERESTING INSIGHTS:

POINTS I'D LIKE TO DISCUSS WITH THE GROUP:

JOURNALING PAGES

Journaling

JOURNALING

Journaling

Journaling

JOURNALING